ON CANADIAN
DEMOCRACY

ON CANADIAN DEMOCRACY

JONATHAN MANTHORPE

Cormorant Books

We acknowledge financial support for our publishing activities: the
Government of Canada, through the Canada Book Fund and The Canada
Council for the Arts; the Government of Ontario, through the Ontario Arts
Council, Ontario Creates, and the Ontario Book Publishing Tax Credit.

LIBRARY AND ARCHIVES CANADA CATALOGUING IN PUBLICATION

Title: On Canadian democracy / Jonathan Manthorpe.
Names: Manthorpe, Jonathan, author.
Description: Includes bibliographical references.
Identifiers: Canadiana (print) 20240317912 | Canadiana (ebook) 20240318013
| ISBN 9781770867543 (softcover) | ISBN 9781770867550 (EPUB)
Subjects: LCSH: Canada—Politics and government—1980- | LCSH: Political
participation—Canada.
Classification: LCC JL65 .M36 2024 | DDC 320.971—dc23

United States Library of Congress Control Number: 2024930461

Series cover design: Angel Guerra
Interior text design: Marijke Friesen
Manufactured by Houghton Boston in Saskatoon,
Saskatchewan in April, 2024.

Printed using paper from a responsible and sustainable resource,
including a mix of virgin fibres and recycled materials.

Printed and bound in Canada.

CORMORANT BOOKS INC.
260 ISHPADINAA (SPADINA) AVENUE, SUITE 502,
TKARONTO (TORONTO), ON M5T 2E4

SUITE 110, 7068 PORTAL WAY, FERNDALE, WA 98248, USA

www.cormorantbooks.com

To Canadian voters,
who need to show that they deserve better.

CONTENTS

INTRODUCTION

AS I WRITE this book, the fate of our Prime Minister's official residence, 24 Sussex Drive in Ottawa, is again in the news. I can't help thinking that in some respects the story of that house is a metaphor for the state of Canadian democracy. The building always was a symbol of a long-gone age and an imported culture. It hasn't represented the reality of contemporary Canada for a long time. But in the last few decades the house has suffered from neglect that has rotted the very foundations of the structure. That neglect has been driven in part by cowardice and fear of voter backlash against spending the money needed to make the repairs that are obviously required. For fifty years no governing party has had the courage to insist that Canada's Prime Minister should live in a safe and draft-free house. As a result, 24 Sussex Drive has become vermin-ridden and uninhabitable.

The governance of our country is fast approaching the same fate, and for similar reasons. But in the case of Canada's political structure, the rot started in the roof and is working its way down to the foundations. The critical failures have been the actions and inactions of our political class and their leaders. They have allowed our politics to become a cultural sibling of sports and reality television game shows. As a result, political parties no longer appeal to the voters on the basis of their policies and the objectives they would pursue in government. Instead, they have adopted the culture of celebrity so that parties identify with the brand of their leader. Party leaders now are chosen not for their abilities as politicians and administrators, but instead for performance skills that can attract public interest at the same level, and sometimes at the same intellectual capacity, as a sports figure or a game show host.

This shift in political culture over the last fifty years is a major contributor to the several factors that have made our Parliament in Ottawa and the legislatures in the capitals of our provinces rather sad irrelevancies. When power comes from the popularity of the leader and not the party, its members, or its policies, then the opposition and the backbenchers — even the government ministers — become little more than a cheering section. Another erosion of our elected assemblies is the elevation of the Supreme Court to an appointed and largely unaccountable agency with the power to interpret laws in such a manner as to subvert the legislative process. The 1982 Charter of Rights and Freedoms removed from the House of Commons much of its authority as the sole representative of the voters on all issues, but most profoundly on social issues. The court, in turn, has become problematically activist.

The justices of the Supreme Court are not the only unelected officials who have an outsized effect on the life of the country. One in five adult Canadians work for the government at one of the three levels: municipal, provincial or territorial, and federal. This is considerably more than in the European Union, the United Kingdom, or the United States. One can argue that Canada is more accurately described as a bureaucracy, in the sense of rule by unelected and largely unaccountable officials, rather than a democracy. The withering of our Parliament and legislatures, the culture of celebrity leadership, and the growing power of the unelected has made it nearly impossible for our elected politicians to steer and direct our bureaucratic establishments, which have become a culture unto themselves that all too often impose their own point of view on public life.

Voters sense the impotence of their elected representatives, especially the backbenchers; some regard the business of elections as a charade. Voter turnout in Canada is nothing to be proud of — falling to 62.3% turnout for the 2021 federal election — and at the level of municipal elections, it is a disgrace. The causes for voter apathy include our "first past the post" voting system, which seldom produces an outcome the majority of electors wanted. But low levels of voter participation in elections only exacerbate the problem of apathy. Should a minority of the population determine the outcome of an election and our governments? A new voting system is needed to better represent the wishes of voters and to encourage voter engagement.

Even though political life of Canada — like many of the democracies of the North Atlantic — is in serious trouble, I do not believe that our institutions and communal brickwork have reached the state of decrepitude as that of the Prime Minister's official residence. The country is not broken. It is not beyond repair. But it requires serious repair. It may even require remaking from the ground up. Take this book, if you like, as a depreciation report. It is a listing of what I think has aged poorly and needs to be replaced or repaired now. It is also a warning of what is to come in the near future, which we should be preparing for now. But it is not a compendium of doom and gloom; at least I hope not. That is not my intention. In every essay, I have set out some options for addressing the problems; or, if those are not obvious, I have put forward aspects that I think Canadians should consider.

This book is written in a mood of indignation, but not anger. I have been a newspaper reporter for almost sixty years and a political reporter for most of that time. An essential commitment for that job is to keep well back from any sort of partisan leanings. The job of a political reporter is to swim in the mainstream of the culture and account to the public on the functioning of the system as events unfold. It is not a political reporter's job to take sides. Political reporters are the Fourth Estate; separate, distinct, and necessarily independent from the other branches of our political system. But, as a close observer and commentator, my indignation does verge on outrage at the way we have allowed our political and social democracy to fall into disrepair since 1968 when Canadian voters first opted for image rather than substance and policy. Having said that, I must add immediately that this series of polemic essays is not an adulation of the good old days. Far from it. Like every past age, some of it was good, some of it was bad, and a lot of it was terrible.

My argument here is that we are not paying enough attention to the way our political, economic, and social institutions are degrading. An added threat is that this comes at a time when democracies world-wide are under assault from authoritarian instincts from within and without. The serious erosions of our civic values and institutions makes us as vulnerable to the assaults of despotism as we have seen in the United States and some of the countries of the European Union. Meanwhile, beyond the bounds of North Atlantic Culture, various brands of what used to be called "enlightened despotism" are taking hold in Asia, the Middle East, Africa, and South America. Citizens in many of those countries seem prepared to accept that they will stay out of politics and avoid dissent, so long as their ruler provides social security and a better standard of living. That deal is not accepted universally, of course. This is why we see continuous flows of people from economically dysfunctional and violent societies heading for what are seen as welcoming, better managed, and safer countries in Europe and North America.

This points to the necessity that the rejuvenation of politics within Canada include a thorough reformation of Canada's stance on the world stage. The occasions when Canada has had to define and defend its national security and national interests have been more limited than in most other countries. Since the prospect of invasion by the United States was removed in the 1860s, the threats to Canadian nationhood have come from internal separatist forces. Canada's status as a nation on the world stage was largely set out and protected for us first by the United Kingdom and then by the US. This bred in Canadians an unrealistic and in some cases dangerously self-delusional view of ourselves and our place in the world. We seldom had to take responsibility for what we said or did. That era of guardianship is now over. Our most recent overseer, the US, is so embroiled in its own internal social and political contest for the nation's soul that it cannot be trusted to honour the obligations it carried in the past. Canadians and their elected representatives need to take a tougher and more clear-headed approach to defining this country's national interests, and to deciding how they are to be defended.

We are also moving into a new age when the way our society works is being refashioned from the ground up by revolutionary technologies. Some hold the promise of huge advances and progress for humanity. But we need to ensure our institutions are fit to defend our values against the intrusions of potentially damaging technologies such as artificial intelligence and the changes in personal behavior they encourage.

Who Canadians are and where they live is also changing radically. This country's agricultural and natural resources continue to form an important economic and cultural backdrop, but Canadians these days are an urban and increasingly metropolitan people. Nearly 83% of Canadians live in cities. That proportion will rise. Reconciliation with First Peoples will continue to change our relationship with the land, calling into question who can do what and where. Reconciliation will change the nature of communal discourse as Indigenous peoples increasingly exercise their own ways of political negotiation and decision-making. Existing Canadian methods and institutions must adapt to work in tandem with Indigenous counterparts. There is no acceptable alternative to some form of cooperative relationship between First Peoples and immigrant communities. We should be open to the prospect that both may have to adjust their ways of doing things for cooperation to be accomplished.

With notable and unfortunate historical exceptions, Canada has welcomed newcomers and absorbed new cultural influences while maintaining the fundamental values of this country's society. Over the decades when most immigrants came from Europe, much of what they found in Canadian society was familiar, making it easy to adapt to living in a new land. The same is true of some waves of immigration from other parts of the world with similar civic values, Hong Kong for example. There has been, however, a changing pattern of immigration in recent decades bringing people from cultures that find Canadian ways entirely strange. By and large, they come to adopt the civic and cultural values of Canada, and accept and are accepted in their new home. But that may not last either for immigrants or citizens born here if the question of what Canada is and who it is for becomes increasingly difficult to answer. Acceptance and assimilation are going to be a mounting challenge if current policies continue to encourage many hundreds of thousands of immigrants to come to Canada every year without the necessary infrastructure, in the broadest sense, being in place.

The argument is that Canada needs to grow its population in order to sustain the economy when the birth rate is low, and Canadians are living longer. That argument has some punch, but there are several other fundamental problems with the Canadian economy that need urgent attention. For years economic productivity — what we get out from the effort put in — has been significantly lower than that of other fully industrialized countries, and it is getting worse. We are becoming an increasingly indolent people. Part of this is a cultural shift as more and more of us decide that our working life must take second place to our private pleasures and pursuits. Part of the reason for that shift is that employers no longer try to make their employees partners in their enterprise as was often the case a generation ago. Canadian businesses need to give their employees more of a financial and collegial stake in their enterprises to stop this slide into mediocrity and to incentivize employees to invest more time and energy. This is also necessary as part of a campaign to reverse the dangerous rise of gross economic disparity between the bulk of the population and the outlandishly wealthy, a situation that began in the 1970s with the adoption of so-called "trickle-down" economic policies in the US and UK, and which spread from there into much of the capitalist world. That and deregulation have for most people removed any hope of improving their standard of living. But this is not a sustainable economic model for the country. Gross disparity and the subservience of employees are urgent problems.

One of the great Canadian virtues is also a vice: our ability to muddle through no matter how seemingly intractable the problems we face. As a virtue, that quality has served us well. Sort of. We still have a military, despite decades of purposeful underfunding. We still have a healthcare service, despite staff shortages and a variety of provincially-designed administrative structures that are not fit for purpose. We still have universities, though in many instances only because they are financially supported by a high proportion of foreign students paying three or four times the fees of those living in-province. We still have a public school system, even though some teachers are having to use go-fund-me campaigns or appeal to parents for money to buy the most basic classroom equipment. As a vice, the ability to muddle through has also allowed us to ignore the reality that we can't muddle through much longer. Canada and the world in which it strives to survive have changed too much for that.

This book is written in a mood of outrage, but it is not a negative rant. Its indignation is based on love and affection, and on years of close-up experience and observation. To accentuate the positive, this polemic puts forward a range of ideas and suggestions for counterattacks against what ails us. Nor is this a call to revolution. Canadians are not natural revolutionaries, though there have been occasions when perhaps they should have been. This treatise is a call for a serious, measured program of reform in almost all aspects of our communal life. To that end, it is a book I hope will prod politicians and members of the decision-making establishment to acknowledge that many of them are living in bubbles increasingly divorced from the lives of the majority of Canadians. But, most of all, I hope that this book sparks discussion among Canadians. We need a national conversation about where this country is going and how it is going to get in shape for the journey.

CHAPTER ONE

Killing Democracy by Neglect

HUMANITY THE WORLD over shares a very short list of hopes and expectations from life. The order of importance, of course, depends on geography, culture, and circumstance. But at the top for most people is the desire for a secure home for themselves and family, whatever form that takes. To sustain home and family there is the need for income of some sort. Until recently, that was usually through a secure job that pays a living wage. People also want to live in a community that shares their culture and values, and with which they are prepared to make a social contract. Then, more broadly for their community or nation, they want security of home, family, work, society, and health. This demands a benevolent government and legal system. Government, whatever form it takes, must therefore fulfill its core responsibilities of regulating the marketplace, suppressing crime, overseeing public health, and ensuring the education of children. This last demand — the education of children — is high up on most people's list wherever they live because a common human passion is that children should have better opportunities and live better lives than their parents.

For much of its recent history, Canada has excelled at meeting the hopes and expectations of its citizens, except, most notably and unforgivably, for the land's First Peoples. But in recent years, Canada has lost the plot. Canadians these days cannot take for granted that this society, one of the leading industrialized and politically sophisticated countries on Earth, can or will meet their core expectations.

Far too many Canadians find it difficult or impossible to keep a roof over their heads. The cost of housing has reached the level where it threatens the very stability of Canadian society. The Canada Mortgage and Housing Corporation (CMHC) will only insure mortgages for a purchase price of $1 million or less; the average cost of a home (house or condominium) in Canada is $657,145; the average price in Toronto is $957,459; and the average price in Vancouver is $1,168,700. CMHC guidelines indicate that people should spend no more than 32% of their gross income on housing and housing costs. But on average, Canadians who do not own their homes outright are spending 46%, and in cities the burden is much, much greater. In Vancouver the cost of rent or mortgages is approaching 80% of income and in greater Toronto it is 72%. What is often forgotten is that the brutally high cost of housing not only diminishes the lives of people forced to pay these outlandish prices, it also impoverishes society as a whole. A society where people must pay upwards of 50% of their income on housing is a drab, dreary, and repellent place destined to become even more so. There is no money for cultural pursuits. There is no money for social gatherings. There is just the drudgery of trying to afford a home and keep food in the fridge. This situation erodes the economy, taking money away from small businesses and putting it all into housing costs.

For a growing number of people, housing of any kind is not something they can aspire to under any circumstances. Statistics Canada says that over the course of recent years around 235,000 people have been homeless at one time or another. On any night in Canada, around 30,000 people are sleeping on the streets or in shelters. Inevitably, these people have gathered into communities of the dispossessed in all of Canada's major cities. The existence of these encampments is a judgement on our failure as a society. It is something of which all Canadians should be deeply ashamed.

There have been radical changes in the workplace, stemming largely from changes in the means of production, business applications of the communications revolution, the ideological passion for deregulation, and the supremacy of investors that spread out from the United States in the 1980s. Trickledown economics with its belief in Darwinian market place forces in lieu of government regulation upset the balance of power and influence in corporate enterprises. There are four partners in any corporate undertaking: the investors, the management, the employees, and the customers. In the 1950s, 60s, and 70s there was a rough balance between the four. The Ronald Reagan and Margaret Thatcher revolutions of the 1980s destroyed that equity. Since then, the majority of corporate power has been firmly in the hands of shareholders and managers. Employees and customers are very much the weak partners. Customers have been compensated by cheap prices for goods as the cost of production has been cut either by technological advances or globalization's access to low-paid labour. Employees, however, now often find that there are few secure jobs around, many don't pay a living wage, and it is rare to find work that offers benefits such as reliable pensions, and health and welfare insurance. One fallout from these changes is that while Baby Boomers — today's grandparents — spent on average twelve years working for one employer, Generation Y, the cohort of young people who entered the job market in 2002, spend only two-and-a-half years in a job. They either bounce from job to job in a hunt for a career they like, become bored with the thankless tasks they have to do to keep a roof over their heads and food on the table, or they face setbacks such as lack of advancement or layoffs. Canadians who are now coming of working age can expect to hold about fifteen different positions in their lifetimes.

Canada used to be a country of unusual equity. To be sure, there were a few very rich families whose wealth came from money garnered and carefully coveted from the early days of exploitation of the country's resources or fruitful opportunities like prohibition in the US. And there were a few who rocketed to economic stardom from some bonanza or other as technologies and society developed in the postwar decades. But for the most part there were few outlandish differences between the incomes and lifestyles of the blue collar and the management classes. That began to change with the recession of the 1980s and 90s. This set off an era of inflation and stagnant expectations for the middle and blue-collar classes from which the country has not recovered. Recent Statistics Canada figures show that the wealthiest 20% of the Canadian population owns over 67% of the country's net worth, while the least wealthy 40% of the population owns just under 3% of Canada's assets. This is inequity at a level that breeds social division and subsequent social unrest.

Failure to address this dangerous disparity is not the only negligence of the federal and provincial governments of all major parties, or that of the country's business and investment classes. For forty years, since the early 1980s when the fashion for Darwinian economics took hold, there has been a steady decline in productivity in Canadian business and a failure to invest in research and development. Between 1984 and 2007, business productivity in Canada fell from 90% of the United States' level to about 76%. Canada's business productivity ranks fifteenth out of eighteen comparable countries, according to the Organization for Economic Cooperation and Development (OECD). By the same token, Canadian investment in research and development fell by 20% in the first decade of this century and has continued to be well below the average measured by the OECD.

One of the factors in Canada's economic stagnation is that it has become a country of monopolies. Federal governments of both major parties have allowed and encouraged the development of a handful of dominant Canadian companies in some industries and retail sectors. This has been done in the name of protecting national industries and culture from the predations of foreign companies. Its main achievement, however, has been to force Canadians to pay outlandish prices for everyday goods and services, and to embed profound inefficiencies into the Canadian economy.

The OECD has said what is clear to most parents. Canadian education continues to fall behind the standards of competitor and partner countries, largely because of a lack of funding, and because education is a provincial responsibility and therefore lacks national standards or goals. Another problem is that more and more Canadian universities and colleges have become dependent on the very high tuition fees charged to international or out-of-province students, mostly because of inadequate public funding. But foreign money is an entry level financial drug. Addiction has led academic institutions to increase the proportion of foreign students it enrolls. These fees are often three or four times the amount Canadians would be charged. One result is that prospective Canadian students are finding it hard to secure places at some universities and colleges in the disciplines they choose. Some go abroad to earn degrees and qualifications, only to find that when they come home, their certificates are not recognized. Acquiring the necessary credentials acceptable to Canadian authorities is often expensive and time-consuming. The dependence on foreign students has also made Canadian universities and colleges vulnerable to unforeseeable events. The closures enforced to combat the COVID-19 pandemic had serious effects on Canadian academia, as have the political crises between Ottawa and India, the People's Republic of China, and Saudi Arabia. All those countries have been major sources of foreign student income for Canadian universities and colleges.

Canadian universities and colleges are also at the forefront of identity politics. They have become a good example of philosopher Karl Popper's proposition in a 1945 essay of the "paradox of tolerance." Popper argued that excessive tolerance inevitably leads to giving power to people who are intrinsically intolerant and who will destroy tolerance. Cancel culture and brutally enforced ideological conformity in Canadian academic institutions are examples and proof of Popper's paradox. We have defended and promoted social liberalism to the point where it has become totalitarian and destructive. In the end, ideological conformity questions the scholarly utility of Canada's colleges and universities.

Some fellow democracies in Europe and the Americas face very serious polarization and frictions among their populations. Canada has not yet been overcome by the same antagonisms, though it can be seen coming at us fast down the political highway. Several surveys show that Canadians are angry and getting more truculent by the day about the depressing state of their lives and the bleak prospects they see in the future. Inflation and economic uncertainty bred by the pandemic spending spree, low interest rates, and Russian President Vladimir Putin's renewed invasion of Ukraine early in 2022 are central elements in the disenchantment of the Canadian public. But there is a broader, deeper unease about the state of the country and uncertainty about the future. Climate change and all its implications for economic wellbeing, health, and the simple security of home and community looms large. But so do other major shifts in the global political order.

The conviction that the US is no longer a dependable ally is of special meaning for Canada. Canadians see themselves alone for the first time as the US shows signs of entering one of its periodic bouts of isolationism. At the same time, the unipolar moment of its global super power dominance is fading with the rise of China and other would-be regional powers. None of these rising powers supports the international order established by the US and its coterie of allies, including Canada, after the Second World War. Countries like China, India, Brazil, Russia, and South Africa want a world order that flows from their own political cultures. That is unlikely to be an inviting climate for Canada and other middle-power democracies.

There is also a noticeable deterioration in the social cohesion of Canada, and clear evidence, especially in large cities, that the contract among Canadians to treat each other with tolerance and courtesy is wearing thin. What is very dangerous is that some political leaders in Canada, at both the federal and provincial level, see an opportunity for personal advancement in these incipient social divisions. They are attempting to promote anger and hatred of others in a fashion that can only be described as evil.

A virtue of democracy is that government does not shout instructions into citizens' faces on an hourly basis. Indeed, most Canadians go weeks and months without having any direct contact with government at all, even though most of us live in places where there are at least three and sometimes four levels of administration. The strength of democracy is that it is adaptable to changing circumstances and the demands of society. The vulnerability of democracy is that it is not in citizens' faces every hour of every day, and that it is very adaptable. When government is not visible and its presence is not felt, it tends to be ignored. People slough off its failings, feel little responsibility for keeping abreast of political issues, and don't bother to vote. Meanwhile, democracy and its institutions morph into different beings. They are living cultures, and if not tended to by the citizenry, they modify themselves. That is what has happened to Canadian political and governmental institutions over the last fifty years. They have become their own beings, their own culture. They are detached from the lives of Canadians in many crucial areas and are no longer responsive to many of the changes that have taken place in Canadian society.

Current public opinion surveys find that at best Canadians are ambivalent about how much trust to put in their governments; at worst, they are downright hostile to the state and many of the institutions that make up the Canadian establishment. An annual survey, the CanTrust Index published by Proof Strategies, is not a hundred percent reliable because it is an online poll and therefore not entirely random. But the 2023 edition is roughly in line with what other polls have found. The index found that just 37% of Canadians trust the federal and provincial governments. That is nothing short of appalling.

There were more grim warnings in some of the detail of the CanTrust Index. The survey found that 56% of Canadians feel that political parties are a "divisive force" in Canadian society. This disenchantment was underlined by responses showing that only 27% of respondents thought politicians "do their best" to serve their constituents. For the most part, Canadians believe that politicians are in the game for their own benefit.

Canadians are equally ambivalent about the trustworthiness of the country's central institutions. The health service, military, and education system scraped support of just over 50%. Others, such as the news media, the Royal Canadian Mounted Police, and the financial markets are in the 40% range. Only 38% of those polled thought Parliament is a trustworthy institution, and just 45% of Canadians have faith in the election process. Residents of the western provinces are markedly less trusting of government and establishment in-stitutions, as are lower-income Canadians. Overall, only just over 40% of Canadians say they are satisfied with the key aspects of their lives.

Canada is not broken, but it is most certainly cracking and creaking at the joints. Canadians have not paid sufficient at-tention to the care, maintenance, and modernization of their society and the political institutions that make it work. The result is not only a loss of public confidence in those insti-tutions, but also in the social and cultural values of democ-racy and the rule of law on which they are based. Canadian democracy and social cohesion may not be under the same immediate threats of destruction as in some other countries, but political disenchantment, economic stagnation, seemingly unstoppable disparity and inequity, and growing indications of social polarization are warnings that Canada has begun the slide down a dangerous path. Now is the time for a clear-eyed identification of what has gone wrong, and a debate on how to fix the institutions that risk becoming dysfunctional, preparing them for the very different world that is racing to-wards us with considerable speed.

One finds no clearer picture of the degradation that is be-setting Canadian democracy and all that flows from it than by looking at the power that has been accumulated around the office of Prime Minister and, to a significant degree, around the provincial premiers. The problem was well set out twenty-three years ago by the former *Globe and Mail* political columnist Jeffrey Simpson in his book *The Friendly Dictatorship*. What he described was a parliamentary system that had degraded into what amounts to an executive presidency overseen by the

Prime Minister and his personal cadre of officials, but without any of the checks and balances written into the US system, for example. The situation has grown much worse since the 2001 publication of Simpson's book. He was writing about the degradation during the period of the Pierre Trudeau, Brian Mulroney, and Jean Chrétien governments. The crumbling of the importance of Parliament, and of the effectiveness of political parties, the parliamentary caucus, and Ministers of the Crown, has accelerated in the two decades since.

Canada has never followed the purist parliamentary system offered by Britain. Because we are a federation, the unitary state model of institutions imported from London had to be bent and contorted into a new and unfamiliar shape. From the start, Canada's Houses of Parliament and the provincial legislatures fashioned forms of parliamentary democracy that were deemed appropriate for this country's social culture, constitutional structure, and economy in the mid-nineteenth century. These are very different from those of the United Kingdom both because of the Canadian reality and because we have been influenced by personality politics and the constitutional form of democracy in the United States. Even so, until perhaps forty years ago, the operation of political party caucuses in Ottawa and the provinces, whether in government or opposition, were far more collegial affairs than they are now. Rank-and-file members of Parliament and the legislatures were recognized as the voices of their constituents, and respected for their local knowledge and understanding. That's how and why they got elected.

There were often members who were acknowledged, through long experience and electoral success, to have a particular understanding of their regions of the country. They were sometimes called "regional barons." Equally, party leaders almost always deferred to ministers or appointed critics on issues within their domains. There were rivalries and intense internal debates, of course. That's the important and constructive nature of democratic politics; but, by and large, there was a collegial basis for the process, even when it got hot and heavy. Behind all that, leaders usually looked to the future of their parties. They prepared for the inevitable successions by mentoring the best among their caucus members so there would be a raft of credible candidates for leadership when the time came. These ways of doing things have largely disappeared right across the political spectrum in Canada. The role of ordinary MPs and MLAs is now hard to fathom, and even government ministers often have little influence with their leaders, and little voice in policy debates affecting their own departments.

All too often, members of party caucuses in Parliament and the legislatures appear to be nothing more than cheering sections in a daily televised reality show. There are efforts by some MPs to reverse this trend and to re-establish the authority and independence of MPs in the House of Commons. Conservative MP Michael Chong stands out as one MP who has pushed for reform on several fronts. What has been extraordinary to witness, however, is the number of MPs, under pressure from their leaders, who have voted against reforms that would have worked to re-establish their influence and freedom to vote according to their conscience. There is no better example than this of the degree to which Parliament has been degraded.

Over the last six decades, celebrity culture has swallowed Canadian political life. Party leaders are selected, not by their colleagues in caucus who know their worth, but by party members nationwide. These members out in the constituencies make their judgement on suitable leaders based on what they see on television and social media. They also tend to be more ideological and less pragmatic than MPs or MLAs. Thus leaders are chosen not for their substance, but for their image and the display they put on. We have seen how disastrous this can be in the selection by the US Republican Party of Donald Trump and his subsequent election to the presidency based on the decisive business leader character he played in the television series "The Apprentice." In reality, Trump was a dodgy flim-flam man, always just one step ahead of creditors and lawyers. Likewise, it was Boris Johnson's television celebrity image — a jolly and eloquent, devoutly patriotic Englishman — that made possible his selection as Britain's Tory party leader and then Prime Minister. But Johnson's true capacities proved to be just as feeble as Trump's, his addiction to lying just as ingrained. He was quickly ousted by the Conservative Party caucus.

Justin Trudeau and Pierre Poilievre are slightly less dramatic products of celebrity culture, but they fit the pattern. Trudeau is a professional performer, and has a performer's ability to respond to the smell of the grease paint and roar of the crowd. He has a well-honed instinct to create the picture and the words craved by the news cycle. But he shows little or no ability or ambition to create a Canada that is fit to confront the more brutal world that is fast approaching. Poilievre has taken another track entirely. He judges that the stress under which very many Canadians are living and the anger this has created is an emotion that can be cultivated and harvested by the Conservatives. Poilievre's playbook is an adaption of that used by Trump in 2016, and his celebrity power is the delivery of masterful phrases of anger that many Canadians see capturing and expressing their own frustrations. Canadians are not by nature a people given to impassioned outrage, but Poilievre is betting that enough of them can be goaded into levels of anger that will push them to vote Conservative. This is a dangerous game. Once public anger is stirred up and unleashed it often attacks its handler and becomes uncontrollable.

A facet of this increasing polarization is that politics is seen as a sporting contest in which winning is everything and any behaviour that smacks of weakness, such as courtesy, is to be avoided at any cost. Sadly, this glorification of locker room machismo means that not only is serious, thoughtful debate and discussion of issues seen as submissive, so is any admission of error. It used to be that politicians resigned when it was clearly shown that they had engaged in immoral, corrupt, or otherwise reprehensible behaviour. Indeed, it was and remains a fundamental truth that democracy is served best when a minister or MP resigns because of unacceptable behaviour. But that doesn't happen any more. MPs and ministers go to any lengths to squirm their way out of taking responsibility for their actions.

No wonder the voting public has so little faith in the honesty and reliability of the people they send to Ottawa or the provincial and territorial capitals.

Canada's political parties have been woefully derelict in confronting and rolling back the celebrity culture and locker room ethics that are doing so much damage to the country's democratic institutions. It's the old story: once a party is in power, it loses the reason and desire to reform the system that got it into office. While out of power, parties have no ability to make changes. Except, that is not quite true. We are dealing here with two distinctly separate political entities. Elected members of Parliament and the legislatures are governed by the rules and laws of those institutions. Political parties out in the country are different entities entirely. They can, to a large degree, make their own rules about how they operate. For example, they can determine how much power the leader and central office have over the operations of constituency branches and the selection of candidates. All Canadian political parties have failed to push back against the dictatorship of the leader and central office. The result is a growing divide between the parties and the voters in the constituencies. It is one of the most serious threats to Canadian democracy. Some close observers and analysts of our political parties argue that it is time for Parliament and the legislatures to set some broad rules for how these institutions operate, much as they do for corporations, charities, and so forth. Regulations restricting voting in leadership contests to citizens and permanent residents are often held up as a necessary boundary for example.

The dangerous dereliction of duty by political leaders to confront and deal with current problems is perhaps no more evident than in the failure to make the Canadian Constitution into a functioning document and process. In 1931 — nearly a century ago — the British parliament asked Canada and the other Dominions to take full responsibility for themselves and their constitutions. Canada dithered for fifty years and finally patriated the constitution in 1982. Since then, there have been half-hearted attempts to create a balance of power between Ottawa and the provinces that will allow the constitution to function and to be amended as circumstances require. Admittedly, this is not an easy agreement to reach, but after the last botched process in 1992 and the failure to get public acceptance of the Charlottetown Accord, no political leader has shown any appetite for trying to amend the Canadian constitution so that it is a better functioning document. This is a serious problem on many fronts. Not least is that one day a political or social emergency will arise that demands co-ordinated federal-provincial action. Ending the role of the British as Canada's head of state comes immediately to mind. But that is impossible, because that role is embedded in the Canadian constitution and will require unanimity among all signatories to change it. That is very unlikely to happen. Even more mundane adjustments to the constitution require Ottawa to gain support from seven provinces comprising over half the Canadian population.

The constitution contains another serious challenge to Canadian democracy and the stature of its legislatures and Parliament: the Charter of Rights and Freedoms, which was attached to the constitution by the government of Pierre Trudeau when the document was patriated in 1982. The effect of the charter is to take responsibility for many social issues out of the hands of Parliament and the legislatures, and to make the Supreme Court the arbiter. This imposed an element of constitutional democracy on a parliamentary democratic system. But the two are fundamentally different approaches to representative and accountable democracy. They are not compatible. The introduction of the Charter was bound to cause problems, and so it has. An attempt was made to assert the supremacy of Parliament and the legislatures by inserting Article 33, the so-called "notwithstanding clause." This allows our elected assemblies to override freedoms embedded in the Charter, but only for a limited period. The hope and expectation was that this opt-out clause would be used only *in extremis*. But it is one of the rules of life that the exceptions rapidly become the norm. Several provinces have now taken to pre-empting Supreme Court challenges to contentious legislation by writing invocations of Article 33 into the legislation from the get-go.

There is very little hope of reverting to the 1960 Bill of Rights that the charter superseded, and returning responsibility for rights and freedoms to the elected representatives of Canadians in Parliament rather than the unaccountable judges of an opaquely appointed court. What hope there is should be explored.

Canadians, understandably, have more faith in the Supreme Court protecting their rights and freedoms than they do in Parliament and the legislatures. A reason for this is that for many voters — usually a majority — Canada's electoral system does not produce the result they wanted. Canada's first-past-the-post system elects the candidate in each constituency who gets the most votes, seldom the majority of votes cast. Thus most elected members have more people who voted against them than for them. Flowing naturally from that, the seats allocated after elections seldom reflect the proportion of votes given to individual parties. Often they are entirely out of whack. To give just one recent example: in the 2022 election in Ontario the Conservatives led by Doug Ford retained power and a majority government by winning seventy of the 124 seats in the legislature. But voter turnout was very low, and it resulted in Ford retaining his majority with the support of only 18% of registered voters.

Canada and the provinces need new electoral systems that more accurately represent the will of the voters in the legislatures, but finding the right alternative is not a simple matter. There is significant public support for proportional representation (PR), of which there are many forms. PR elections aim to allocate seats in the legislature or parliament based on the proportion of votes cast for each party. This sounds good. It sounds democratic, but there are many serious problems with how PR functions. PR systems produce a host of minority parties that have to be welded into a governing coalition. The reality is that coalition building often results in giving undue influence and power to fringe parties or fundamentalists.

There is a stronger argument to be made in favour of minor reforms to Canada's existing first-past-the-post system so that election outcomes better reflect the will of voters while still producing a centrist, workable parliament and government.

The 2022 Ontario election also highlights another issue, and that is the declining number of Canadians who go to the polls, whether it is for federal, provincial, or municipal elections. In recent decades voter participation in federal elections has bumped along in the mid-sixty percent range, which means that about a third of eligible voters don't cast ballots. Despite this, successive federal governments have not considered this gap enough of a problem to warrant serious attention. Voter turnout is persistently lower in provincial and municipal elections. Taking into consideration that these are the levels of government that most directly affect people's lives, public apathy should be taken a good deal more seriously than it is.

Increased voter participation has to be a central element in the revival and sustenance of Canadian democracy. It is a simple proposition that citizens need to play their part in ensuring the survival of the rights and liberties guaranteed by parliamentary democracy, which they enjoy. But democracy is not only about rights; it is also about responsibilities. Of the 199 countries and territories in the world that hold elections, twenty-seven have compulsory voting laws and substantially higher voter turnout at elections as a result.

For generations, Canadians have been inclined to regard political and business dealings in their country as among the world's least corrupt. Canadian history is heavily pockmarked by the stories of crooks and scammers in both politics and business, of course, but they have been the exception rather than the rule. Public life and business in Canada have been ruled by common decency, a sense of honest dealing, and probity. At least that is the way Canadians have seen it. We are beginning to be not so sure. The annual corruption perception index put together by the German-based anti-corruption organization, Transparency International, finds that Canadians are looking around and becoming less certain that their country is a haven of honest dealing. It has come as a shock for Canadians to be told their country is one of the global centres for money laundering by drug and human traffickers, and corrupt officials and business people from authoritarian states like Russia and the People's Republic of China.

This money laundering underworld, aided by Canadian lawyers, accountants, and banks, surfaced when the waves of money coming in from China, Russia, Latin America, and other unstable regions set off an explosion in the Canadian property market. Canada had no serious legal defences against the onslaught and is struggling to work out how to address and erase the widespread corruption that threatens to take root. The sort of people who feel the need to hide assets in benign countries like Canada are also the sort of people who do not hesitate to use corruption to get what they want in all aspects of their lives. There are some signs that Ottawa and the provinces are starting to take the situation seriously. The Financial Transactions and Reports Analysis Centre (FINTRAC), which as its name suggests was established as a centre for information gathering rather than an investigation and enforcement outfit, has begun to reach out for culprits. In December 2023 alone it levied a $1.3 million penalty against the Canadian Imperial Bank of Commerce and a $7.4 million fine against the Royal Bank of Canada. In both cases the banks were fined for failing to comply with rules and regulations aimed at preventing money laundering and the financing of terrorism. But much more needs doing to erase Canada's reputation as a cleanser of dirty money.

From some perspectives, Canada is not so much a country as a loose association of antagonistic and predatory governments and administrative bodies all competing to make life as frustrating and complicated for their citizens as possible.

Provincial and territorial governments have the most direct effect on the daily lives of Canadians, but all thirteen of these authorities glory in their regional individuality and accentuate these differences whenever possible. Because of the nature of the Canadian federation, opportunities for the provinces to display their individuality are extensive. It can be taken for granted that almost everything that involves provincial definition or administration is different in its detail across the country. Some of these differences are just petty amusements, such as the complex rules and regulations governing who is allowed to sell what alcohol, and when and where they are allowed to do so. Others have far greater impact on the functioning of the country, such as the lack of national educational standards and uniform approaches to healthcare. Behind the provincial governments are legions of provincially mandated crown corporations with varying degrees of transparency that are appointed to oversee all manner of matters affecting people's lives.

There are many old ways of doing things in Canada, often born of the country's British heritage and its predominantly European population, and these are being questioned. That questioning is likely to grow more intense and lead to demands for change. The countries and regions from which people immigrate to Canada have changed significantly in the past few decades. Asia, the Middle East, and Africa are now the places from which most of Canada's new immigrants come. They come, of course, because they are attracted to what they have been told about the security and opportunity of life in Canada, and the civic values that sustain those attractions. It is inevitable, however, that the new Canadians will change the cultural context of Canada even as they join the efforts to sustain its fundamental values. It is also true that more and more immigrants are finding that Canada is not living up to its billing. Many are leaving at the first opportunity.

The argument goes that Canada needs more people to maintain and grow its economic well-being. The current government plans to encourage the immigration of about 500,000 people a year. Statistics Canada estimates that this will result in the population growing from its current forty million people to around fifty million by 2050. The agency also expects that by 2041 about two-in-five Canadians will come from what it calls a "visible minority group."

Clearly, the successful absorbing of this many people every year is going to be a massive task. There are the straightforward practical issues of providing enough housing, schools, jobs, healthcare, and other bits of the framework for these people's new lives. So while it is Ottawa that dictates how many new Canadians are admitted, it is the provinces that have to provide and manage the infrastructure. There are also the more complex matters of helping immigrants feel confidently at home in a country with an unfamiliar language, culture, and governmental institutions. Canadians have considerable experience with these matters, but that expertise is going to be tested by the sheer volume of newcomers if government plans go ahead.

There is another profound restructuring of Canadian society in the offing, and that comes from the ongoing movement for reconciliation with the land's Indigenous Peoples. The 2015 Truth and Reconciliation Commission proposed ninety-four actions needed to achieve a new and sustainable relationship between Canada's Indigenous peoples and the settlers, mostly from Europe, who have come to live in this country since the early 1600s. By and large, Canadians have begun to acknowledge past wrongs, but there is no unified response across the country. There is an active process of reconciliation in British Columbia and northern Canada. That process is organic, which is as it should be. Indigenous communities are exercising their rights to social and political self-governance, with practices based on their traditional cultures. These will lead to clear self-determination within the communities and a new compact in Canada. But there can be dangers in the high velocity of change. The backlash in New Zealand, starting in late 2023 when a conservative government was elected and began rolling back concessions to the Maori people of the islands, is a warning. To succeed, reconciliation needs to be a mainstream movement.

My observation over the past year or so is that Canadians are increasingly aware of the problems with the country's democracy and its political life in general. There is a grassroots movement under way that is producing only a low hum of warning at the moment. But evidence of this movement can be seen in the steady flow of news stories and commentaries in newspapers and magazines, broadcast interviews, and social media chatter about the issues raised in this book. It is evident too in the discussions by such groups as the Canadian Club, Probus, Rotary, book clubs, *koffeeklatsch*, Legion bars, and the myriad other places where Canadians discuss the state of their world. Political leaders would do well to see that reform at many levels of Canada's political life is necessary now while it is still controllable.

Ultimately, these questions and their potential answers will surface in elections and, if candidates are listening, those will produce MPs and MLAs who are willing to adjust the set of Canada's sails and the course she is on; but, for that to happen, members of our elected assemblies and the political parties they represent have to regain control of the political agenda.

In order to move forward, they must confront the first hurdle to change: the fact that we are living in what amounts to an elected dictatorship.

CHAPTER TWO

Toppling the Elected Dictatorship

CANADIANS GIVE THEIR prime minister more unquestioned power than the citizens of any other leading democracy. Canadian government leaders have far more unhindered freedom to rule than presidents of the United States, prime ministers of the United Kingdom, or leaders in almost any other parliamentary democracy. The powers Canadians give to their prime ministers are so many, varied, and beyond accountability that it is immediately understandable why political analysts have used phrases such as "imperial democracy" and "friendly dictatorship" to describe the reality of the Canadian system.

Looking at that list of powers, it is a wonder that international organizations monitoring the health of democracies continue to place Canada as high in the rankings as they do. In 2023, *The Economist* Intelligence Unit, the research arm of the magazine, placed Canada twelfth in its rankings of world democracies, sandwiched between Uruguay and Luxembourg in an index where the Nordic nations, New Zealand, Switzerland, and Taiwan cornered the top ten. Other organizations such as the right-wing Freedom House in the US and Sweden-based International Institute for Democracy and Electoral

Assistance continue to judge Canada a top-notch democracy. These organizations, of course, tend to look at what happens in the run-up to and during elections, not what they produce. What Canadian national elections actually produce is a leader with powers that can be compared with those of an eighteenth century European monarch. One or two Canadian Prime Ministers have been called "the Sun King" for this very reason.

The extraordinary number of Canadian prime ministerial powers fall into two main categories. The first is the ability of the Prime Minister, backed by his or her staff in the Prime Minister's Office (PMO) and the Privy Council Office (PCO), to direct and control what happens in government and in parliament. The second is the astonishing unchecked power of patronage Canadians give their prime minister to appoint all the leading figures in the country's public life, judiciary, and administration.

These powers have become even more potent in recent decades as the culture of celebrity leadership has taken hold. As a result, demands for accountability that should come from Parliament have eroded into dust. A key part of this process is that Canadian prime ministers have become surrounded by a praetorian guard of powerful and often intimidating political agents and civil servants. The PMO is made up of the Prime Minister's partisan courtiers whose role is to promote and sustain his political success. It is often their role to be menacing and demanding so that the Prime Minister doesn't have to dirty his hands. The job of the PCO, staffed by civil servants, is to ensure that the government ministries and their armies of officials follow and achieve the Prime Minister's policy agenda. The PCO is inhabited by the brightest and best from among the members of the civil service, and is also the place where likely candidates for advancement are placed on temporary secondment to test their mettle. It is a highly competitive organization that is also an exclusive club of the favoured. PCO officials are constantly looking over the shoulders of government ministers, and often have more influence about what happens in a department than does the elected MP assigned as minister.

Sometimes, of course, when the system produces a prime minister who is not up to the job, the question arises about whether the government is actually being run by officials and party hacks in the PMO and PCO.

The groups that oversee ministries can become heavily overcrowded. The deputy minister in each department — the senior civil servant charged with making the ministry run efficiently and in the direction the government wants — is a civil servant chosen by the Prime Minister. Unlike in other parliamentary democracies such as Britain, it is very common in Canada to see a new government of a new political stripe remove deputy ministers appointed by the previous regime and replace them with people politically in line with the new Prime Minister. This Canadian practice undermines the credibility of the civil service as a non-partisan body working for the public good, no matter the political character of the government.

The British have taken a step towards trying to remove this partisan politicization of the civil service. In London, the Civil Service Commission regulates recruitment into the Civil Service and tries to ensure appointments are made based on merit after fair and open competition. When there is a vacancy for a deputy minister post, known in Britain as the Permanent Secretary, the commission interviews qualified candidates and gives a list to the Prime Minister from which to choose. Thus, the Prime Minister has the final say, but the system does at least establish that a candidate's qualifications and experience are the first requirement, not his or her partisan appeal.

The Prime Minister's patronage power really comes into its own outside Parliament. It starts with the de facto head of state, the Governor General. This in itself is extraordinary, bordering on the bizarre. The Head of State represents Canadian sovereignty and the soul of the nation well beyond the limits of politics. That this symbol of the nation should be chosen by one politician defies sanity, not least because there are moments in the life of any parliamentary democracy when the head of state has to make profound political choices. This usually happens when no party wins a majority in an election and it falls to the Governor General to decide who to ask to form a government. It is a moment when the country needs to have absolute trust that the Governor General's choice is not a repayment for past favours. And yet, since this appointment devolved to Canada with the Statute of Westminster in 1931, the post of head of state has remained a gift of the Prime Minister. Prime Ministers of both major parties have never shrunk from using this power of appointment to bolster their own views on the nature of Canada, which have sometimes been at odds with the perspective of the country's mainstream.

In 2012, then-Prime Minister Stephen Harper made a stab at removing the smell of patronage from the process.

He established the Advisory Committee on Vice-Regal Appointments, which was given the responsibility of vetting candidates for both the post of Governor General and of Lieutenants Governor for the provinces. Harper was criticized for appointing a "tight circle of monarchists" to be members of the committee. They consulted widely with various groups across the country and produced a list of five candidates for the Governor General's post for Harper. He chose David Johnston, an academic who had an association with the Trudeau family, but also history with the Conservative Party.

Johnston led an inquiry into the Airbus Affair in the 1980s in which Prime Minister Brian Mulroney was accused of accepting bribes from the European airline manufacturer competing to supply Air Canada. Mulroney emerged unscathed. After this one outing, whose outcome raised some eyebrows, Harper's vice-regal selection committee was disbanded by the Liberals when they returned to power under the leadership of Justin Trudeau in 2015. Trudeau's first choice without the help of a committee was disastrous. He picked former astronaut Julie Payette, who resigned after allegations of a toxic work environment at Rideau Hall. After her resignation in 2021, Trudeau was heavily criticized for not having her properly vetted. He appointed a six-member panel called the "Advisory Group on the Selection of the Next Governor General." This ad hoc group came up with a shortlist from which Trudeau chose the Inuit activist and advocate Mary Simon, who became Canada's first Indigenous Governor General.

There have been arguments made in the past that the Governor General should not be an object of partisan patronage. It has been suggested that the Governor General, or at the very least the candidates for that post, should be chosen in private by a parliamentary committee. Perhaps Canada should go the whole hog and have the House of Commons, as the elected representatives of the Canadian people, pick the Governor General. A system that might work would be to have a parliamentary committee or, as in Harper's time, an advisory committee, put forward two vetted candidates. Members of Parliament could then have a free vote by secret ballot. There are many other ways in which the Governor General could be chosen that would be more communal than continuing to allow the head of state to be the choice of one person, the prime minister. The task could be given to a reformed Senate, or it could be assigned to the provincial premiers and heads of territorial governments as representatives of Canada's diversity. Governors General could even be selected by a committee of members of the Order of Canada chosen by lottery.

One thing is certain: the Governor General should not be directly elected by Canadian voters. There has been a huge argument about this in Australia, where the republican movement to ditch the British monarchy is far more active than in Canada. That move has always gone off the rails because Australian voters want to pick their head of state, and the country's politicians want to make the selection themselves. The politicians are right. A head of state with his or her own political legitimacy bestowed by the voters is a recipe for serious difficulties and perhaps disaster in a parliamentary system. When there is no clear majority in the House of Commons and it falls to the Governor General to choose someone to be Prime Minister and form a government, there is no room for a head of state with political legitimacy rivalling that of the House of Commons. It would be much better if the Governor General is chosen by MPs or a parliamentary committee.

It is a similar story with the Prime Minister's power to appoint the justices of the Supreme Court. There have been efforts, by Stephen Harper in particular, to involve parliamentary committees in the selection and vetting of candidates for the Supreme Court. But the committees had no veto power. The selection of Supreme Court judges remains the prerogative of the prime minister. In the same way, the Prime Minister appoints the head of the Canadian military, the Chief of the General Staff, and other key senior officials including the Auditor General, the Information Commissioner, and the Ethics Counsellor. Also at the Prime Minister's patronage are the heads of crown corporations of which there are about fifty. These bodies and the leading positions at the Prime Minister's bequest include the Canadian Broadcasting Corporation, the Bank of Canada, the Canada Council for the Arts, Export Development Canada, the National Capital Commission, the Royal Canadian Mint, and Via Rail.

Again, the British have addressed this issue, and again with only marginal success. The post of Commissioner for Public Appointments has been created, supported by independent assessors, to judge candidates for senior posts in crown corporations, which the British call "quangos," short for "quasi autonomous non-government organizations." But the final decision on appointments to quangos still rests with the minister in charge of the department that oversees the arms-length body. There have been recommendations in Britain that the whole business of selecting senior staff for quangos be taken entirely out of ministerial hands and given to an independent "National Appointments Commission." Ministers would retain responsibility for setting out the role of these extra-governmental public bodies, and the qualifications for managerial board members, but the commission would make appointments based on the merit of the candidates. There is also a suggestion that, rather like in the US, select committees of Parliament should have the authority to hold hearings to vet proposed appointees to quangos and reject candidates of whom they disapprove for one reason or another.

In any event, there are better, cleaner, and more open ways of choosing people to run what are some of this country's most important and influential institutions beyond the current system of secret conclaves in the Prime Minister's Office.

Some of the Prime Minister's powers of appointment directly involve the working of Parliament. There is the appointment of Cabinet Ministers and Members of the Senate, of course, but there are also other positions that influence the way Parliament works that in Canada, though not in other democracies, are under the patronage of the Prime Minister. The most pernicious is the allocation and appointment of the chairs of parliamentary standing committees. An attempt was made to change this in 2002 when the standing orders were changed to require the election of committee chairs. But the party whips have taken control of the process by ensuring that only candidates acceptable to the party leaders get nominated. More than that: as it is not a secret ballot, the whips know who, if anyone, voted against the Prime Minister's candidate. MPs know that defying government whips too often blocks their route to advancement. This leaves the impression and sometimes the reality that these committees, whose job it is to examine and question government policies and actions, are under the thumb of the Prime Minister.

That the Prime Minister's authority is supreme and un-questionable is clearly seen in another appointment. The Clerk of the House is the chief lawyer for Parliament with the responsibility of giving legal and procedural advice to the MPS as members of the House of Commons, and therefore distinct from their membership in the government and the po-litical parties. In most parliaments it is the Speaker, the chair of the House of Commons selected by the MPS, who appoints the Clerk of the House. Not in Ottawa. In Ottawa the Prime Minister and the PMO appoint the Clerk of the House.

In 2001 the system was dressed up to look slightly less intrusive than in the past. Now, the government puts forward someone to be appointed to the clerk's position. This is put to the Standing Committee of Procedure and House Affairs, which has thirty days to consider the proposal, at the end of which it must report to the House of Commons. The House then votes on the committee recommendation without debate or amendment. As even minority governments manage to keep control of committees, the reality of this system is that the Clerk of the House is an appointment in the Prime Min-ister's patronage. That is not a good look for a parliament whose members are supposed to retain a high degree of inde-pendence on many issues.

Just look at the contrast with the way the Australian and British parliaments appoint their clerks. For the Australians, "the Clerk, an impartial servant of the House, is appointed by the Speaker after the Speaker has consulted Members of the House about the proposed appointment. In practice, party leaders are consulted." That's how the Australian House of Representatives, as they call their parliament, describes the process. The appointment is a matter for the House and is members only. The government is not involved.

The British take a slightly different approach, but again, it is a matter for the House of Commons and not the government. In Westminster there is a selection panel that interviews candidates. The panel is chaired by the Speaker and includes the House Leaders of the governing and opposition parties. Because the clerk, as well as being the legal adviser to the MPs, is also the chief executive managing the functioning of the House of Commons, trades unions and bodies overseeing workplace equity also get to offer their opinions on candidates. Optics matter in this process, and in Canada, the image is of a Parliament totally under the thumb of whoever happens to be prime minister.

The role of the Speaker, and the stature of Parliament along with it, has been diminished in other ways. One important power, certainly as it affects the public perception of Parliament gained from Question Period, is control over who asks questions. To the viewers at home, Question Period may look like high drama, but in reality the whole thing is orchestrated. In most parliamentary democracies, members of parliament who want to ask a question of a minister catch the eye of or send a note to the Speaker, who then recognizes them and gives them the floor to speak. At least in principle, this system says that the job of the House of Commons is to question the government about its policies and actions, and to hold it accountable for the outcomes and its mistakes. Not in Canada. In Ottawa, this authority has been taken from the Speaker. Instead, the party whips put together lists of their members who want to ask questions. These are negotiated and then sorted into an agenda, which is delivered to the Speaker. Question Period is orchestrated in the PMO.

The ideal of a parliamentary democracy is that members are elected primarily to represent their constituents and should have the freedom to pursue that duty, even if it clashes with party or government policies. In other parliamentary democracies, it is common for MPs to refuse to accept orders from government or party whips to vote the way leaders want if the issue at hand involves conscience or is beyond partisan politics. One of the reasons the bill to patriate the Canadian constitution from Britain got held up in the British Parliament in 1981 and 1982 was because British MPs still have a high degree of independence. Even a prime minister with the authority of Margaret Thatcher knew that she couldn't demand unquestioning support for the bill from her Tory backbenchers on a constitutional issue. British MPs consider constitutional matters their domain, where the leader should not try to demand party loyalty. Prime Minister Pierre Trudeau and the officials in his office were astonished and incredulous when they came up against this very different parliamentary culture forty years ago. For then, as now, MPs in Canada, especially on the government benches, are simple spear carriers in the legions of the Prime Minister. They go where directed, and snarl, clap, or cheer as the stage manager demands. To a significant degree, this is because they all know who got them elected; on whose coattails they rode to

Ottawa. The reason for this is the celebrity culture that has taken over Canadian politics, especially at the national level, but also in many of the provinces.

Political parties are now defined by the public's perception of their leader. A political party's brand is not so much the policies it espouses as it is the public image of the leader. This is a very dangerous development born of the age of visual communication. It is a gift for charlatans and demagogues. No better evidence is the election to national leadership of Boris Johnson in Britain and Donald Trump in the United States. Both men were swept into power because enough voters thought they were supporting the characters both men played on television. In both cases the TV characters played by Johnson and Trump bore little or no relationship to reality.

Former Conservative Party leader Erin O'Toole summed up his view of what has happened to parliament in a speech in the House of Commons in June 2023. "Performance politics is fuelling polarization," he said. "Virtue signalling is replacing discussion. And far too often we are just using this chamber to generate clips, not to start national debates."

Another factor keeping MPs in line is that in recent decades prime ministers and other party leaders accept or reject candidates nominated by party constituency associations. In essence, this has disenfranchised party organizations at the local level, at least if they try to nominate a candidate unacceptable the party leader. This degrading of the purpose of riding associations has been compounded by rules deterring them from putting up rival candidates against sitting members.

The accumulation of extraordinary power in the hands of Canadian prime ministers over the last fifty years or so has inevitably led to ethical corruption. Canadian prime ministers no longer feel the need to be accountable to the Canadian public; to accept responsibility for their actions and to resign if they have breeched what is normally considered ethical behaviour. The contrast with Britain is profound. There Boris Johnson was ousted by his own backbench Conservative MPs because of his inability to tell the truth about almost anything. He was also hauled before a House of Commons ethics committee to face allegations that he and his staff had breached his own government's restrictions on social gatherings during the COVID-19 pandemic.

More than that, Johnson had then lied to the House of Commons about the incidents. In late 2023, Johnson was still going through the wringer of investigation by a parliamentary committee into his actions while the tenant of 10 Downing Street. Donald Trump was not brought to heel in the same way, but he was impeached by the House of Representatives twice. He was only saved because when tried in the Senate, the votes to remove him from office did not reach the required two-thirds majority. He still faces accountability for paying off a porn star with whom he had an affair, a multitude of charges and court cases in various jurisdictions over his attempts to overthrow the results of the 2020 election, and his absconding from the White House with scores of highly classified documents.

That sort of thing doesn't happen in Canada. Prime ministers are never held to account for ethically questionable actions. Perhaps worst of all, backbenchers in the House of Commons no longer see themselves primarily as representatives of the people who elected them, and therefore owing prime loyalty to the interests of their constituents. Canadian MPs see loyalty to their party and its leader as their duty beyond any other. A 2020 study by the Samara Centre for Democracy found that Canadian MPs vote as they are instructed by their party whips 99.6% of the time. No wonder the Canadian public has such a jaundiced view of the quality and motives of MPs. An Angus Reid poll in November 2023 asked respondents to describe the sentiments that came to their minds when they watched sessions of the House of Commons. "Posturing" was the top reaction that came to mind for 54% of those polled. 46% thought the whole business was "useless," and 38% found the performances "dishonest." An interesting and perhaps encouraging product of the poll was that it showed that over half (57%) of Canadians watched televised parliamentary proceedings sometimes and a sizable minority are regular viewers. The downside of that is that they are not impressed at all by what they see. Across the country, at least 70% of Canadians said they don't believe individual MPs have any power or influence, that they simply follow the instructions of their leader, and that there is no real debate in parliament on current issues.

The imbalance of power and influence that has grown between the prime minister and both houses of parliament needs to be reversed. A new relationship needs to be established in which the prime minister is beholden to the House of Commons and which reaffirms the role of MPs as primarily the representatives of their constituents, and whose voices have political legitimacy. This can be achieved in a number of ways. An obvious and important one is to change the way party leaders are chosen.

Canada was an early convert to the politics of celebrity which welled up in the age of television, but which also seeped over the border from the US where the culture of the leader and the sanctity of individual rights have always dominated. This is a sharp contrast with the historic Canadian political culture of communal rights and responsibilities. One influence from the US is that party leaders are chosen by constituency delegates at national conventions. It is easy to understand why these often dramatic pieces of made-for-television razzmatazz were adopted by Canadian political parties under pressure from party organizers. They were attention magnets and usually gave the party a boost in public opinion polls. But they were not a sensible way to choose a leader in a parliamentary democracy, and the fallibility has become even more intense as some parties have adopted online selection of leaders by the entire party membership.

Now, democracy in the age of instant communication demands that rank-and-file party members in the constituencies have a hand in the selection of new party leaders. These days, that voting is more likely to happen online, rather at in-person gatherings where grassroots members mingle in one of Canada's majestic railway hotels. A vote by all party members looks more democratic than the old delegate conventions, but unless the selection of candidates is based on the primary involvement of the party's parliamentary caucus it is not an improvement. Indeed, a feature of leadership contests these days is activists hustling around to sign up new party members to vote for their candidate. There are often questions about who has paid for the new memberships and whether these new members have any real interest in the party or the candidate beyond their immediate financial gain. The same questions arise when there are contests to be a party's election candidate and the outcome hangs on how many new members a candidate can sign up.

Let's remember for a moment what a prime minister is. A prime minister is a member of the House Commons who can gather and hold enough support from fellow members to be able to form a government. And that person can remain prime minister only so long as he or she retains the support of the majority of the House of Commons members. In Canada, the caucus support of some parties has influenced potential candidates' decisions on whether or not to run for leadership. In 2008, for example, some well-qualified potential candidates for the leadership of the federal Liberal Party stepped aside when it became known that 70% of the caucus supported the writer and academic Michael Ignatieff. He proved to be a disastrous choice. Perhaps a more formal contest in the parliamentary party, as happens in parliamentary democracies elsewhere, would have allowed some of the other candidates to make their mark.

A series of ballots among parliamentary caucus members could produce two or three candidates to put to the national party membership for the final selection of a new leader. A two-stage system like this would affirm that the leader is beholden to the caucus, not the other way around. This would change the relationship in parliament in favour of the MPs. In Westminster, when the Conservative Party needs a new leader, the caucus goes through a series of secret ballots to come up with two candidates. Those two names are then put to party members out in the constituencies who pick the winner. This means that the two candidates usually have strong support and backing in caucus. It doesn't always work, as the turmoil in the British Conservative Party after the Brexit referendum in 2016 shows. There is a similar system in Australia where MPs have a central role in selecting candidates for the leadership. To reinforce the role of the MPs, a proposal is being considered that on the final ballot for the new leader, the caucus members' votes have equal weight as those of the party rank and file. Thus to win leadership, a candidate would need the support of more than half the caucus and a majority of members of the party.

Equally important is how to remove a leader who for one reason or another has lost the support of the caucus or the party, but who refuses to leave. In the parliamentary system it should not be the leader who decides whether they are going to continue at the helm. It should be the decision of the caucus. All the parties have leadership review mechanisms, most of which kick in after an election and which are conducted at party conventions. By and large they work well enough. There have been no major replays of the drama it took to get John Diefenbaker out of the leadership of the Progressive Conservative Party in 1967 after a large faction of the party decided he was well past his sell-by date. It took the party years to recover from the friendships and associations that were shattered in that turmoil. This upheaval also meant that for close to two decades the voters found it impossible to see the Conservatives as a credible governing party. Thus it would give a healthy rebalance to the relationship between leaders and the parliamentary parties if members of the caucus had a mechanism at hand to remove an unpopular or ineffective leader. It is, after all, the caucus members who see the leader performing in the back rooms every day.

A good idea can be taken to excess, however. In Australia's parliament in Canberra, as well as in the country's state legislatures, members of a caucus can at any time challenge the leadership and call for a vote. This is known colloquially as a "spill." Until very recently, it only required a simple majority of caucus members to call for the ousting of the leader for it to be successful. When this happens, it is said, again colloquially, that the leader has been "rolled." Between 1970 and 2015 there were 72 leadership "spills," including those in Australian state legislatures. The ditching of federal party leaders and prime ministers has become increasingly popular in this century. Five prime ministers were ousted in spills between 2010 and 2018, when Scott Morrison evicted and replaced the conservative Liberal Party Prime Minister Malcolm Turnbull. Former Labour Party Prime Minister Kevin Rudd, who was ousted by his deputy Julia Gillard in 2012, then spilled and rolled her the following year to regain the prime ministership.

Rudd tried to get his party to require a 75% vote in favour of the ouster for it to work, but without immediate success. A decade later, Australian parties are edging towards a compromise by which a leadership challenge would need the support of two-thirds — 66% — of the caucus. As can be seen by the frequency with which Australian party leaders have been spilled and rolled in the last few years, the fifty-percent-plus-one rule is too easy. Bad showing in the polls in the Sunday newspapers can see a leader gone by Monday lunchtime. But a leader who cannot muster support from two-thirds of the caucus should clearly be rolled out the door.

As well as being a servant of parliament and of their party's caucus, prime ministers and opposition party leaders should be servants of their political parties. Political parties, however, are not what they once were. The increasing sophistication of political polling and marketing strategies — sometimes more imagined than real — have usurped much of the mechanics of political organization and campaigning. Party headquarters and the leader's office now have the tools at hand and under their own control to direct and steer the operation. Squadrons of party members out in the boonies reporting on the mood in their constituency, passing on information about rising issues or intelligence about what is going on in the other parties, and in turn spreading the word from party headquarters to their friends and neighbours are seen as largely unnecessary and obsolete.

Until relatively recently, the numerical strength of local party membership gave a reasonable thumbnail picture of the strength of the party as a whole. Vibrant constituency associations spoke of local involvement, of ideas and influence bubbling up from the grassroots, an army of workers ready to join the ranks of election campaigns, and, of course, fundraisers willing and able to grease the wheels of the party juggernaut. Canadians wishing to be personally involved in politics, however, have got the message that in their political interests, as for some of them at their workplace, they have been made redundant by technology. Canadians have concluded that the party establishments have little interest in hearing directly from citizens with their thoughts and observations. Pollsters and focus groups tell parties what people are thinking. So people are staying away in droves from formal association with political parties. Fewer than 2% of Canadians now belong to political parties, and it is this 2% who choose party leaders under the existing systems.

The response by political parties to the disengagement not only of people who would once have been local activists, but of the Canadian citizenry in general, has been put down to apathy. The parties' response has been to redouble their efforts to use the abilities of their marketing technologies to target voters at election times with finely crafted and personalized messages of solidarity. What political parties have failed to grasp is that Canadians have disengaged from participating in politics, and are increasingly hesitant to vote because they feel themselves unwelcome outsiders in the world of politics and government. Surveys of Canadians show they are not apathetic about politics, far from it. But they feel that they are excluded from the whole process. More than that, the belief has taken hold among many Canadians that the political system is not working with their concerns or interests in mind.

An excellent example of the disdain that political parties now hold for Canadian voters is the effort put into arranging the televised all-candidates debates at election times. These are not debates in any serious sense of the word, nor are they any kind of tribute to a wholesome political process. These events are much more closely related to televised game shows and reality programs than they are a real effort to give Canadians information that will help them decide how to cast their ballots. The premise of these debates is that there might be a gotcha moment when one party leader or another comes up with a clever retort that decides the election.

This is no way to run a democracy. It is an insult to everyone involved. Television, streaming, and social media are undoubtedly the most important carriages for political news and information these days. But emulating game shows for political programming is not a proper use of the media. It would be far more positive, productive, and respectful if panels of experienced and well-prepared interviewers drawn from all aspects of the media (and perhaps academia and civil society) had hour-long interviews with each of the party leaders. Then voters might learn something about them, how they think, and what they propose. The debates, as currently constituted, give a superficial and false picture of the leaders and their parties. They play into and reinforce the culture of celebrity politics.

The negative results of Canada becoming an elected dictatorship with a neutered parliament are deep and profound. One response has been to try to bolster other levels of government with additional power or influence, or add new institutions in order to counterbalance the power of the prime minister. We will look at these efforts, but they have not succeeded and I don't believe they can while parliament and the prime minister are in a dysfunctional relationship. As I have written and assembled these essays, I have become convinced that the key to unlocking the barriers to repairing our democracy is to dismantle this electoral system that revolves around the celebrity and curb appeal of a handful of individuals. If Ottawa worked as it should — if it worked as a representative system based on discussion and resolution of communal issues — then the other problems with the Canadian polity and federation can be overcome. In a country of immense diversity, no other democratic model will work. Fundamentally, the overriding problem for Canadian democracy is the unaccountable power that has been gathered into the hands of the prime minister. Until that problem is addressed and redressed, until a sustainable working relationship between the prime minister and parliament is restored, no tinkering with the other levels of our institutions will work.

It is going to take sustained effort and pressure by MPs and MLAs to make this an issue that can't be ignored. Even with that, in the end, it is going to take backing from a prime minister who is willing to give up the untrammeled hold on power.

CHAPTER THREE

Caligula's Horse

THE ESSENTIAL QUESTIONS of what the Senate does and who does it have been spiky issues since Canada was created. We have inherited our notion of the purpose of the Senate from the constant repetition of a remark by Canada's first prime minister, Sir John A. Macdonald, that it should be like Britain's House of Lords, a chamber of sober second thought. But Sir John A. was doing his best to create a unitary state, with minimal doffing of the hat to federalism. He wanted and, in the end, largely succeeded in importing off-the-shelf the British model of politics and administration. The Atlantic colonies were deeply suspicious and wary of Sir John's objectives. They wanted the Senate to be, similar to its namesake in the United States, an upper house the purpose of which was to represent the interests of the regions in the Canadian partnership. That desire has never been fulfilled, and now it probably never will be. The anxieties of the provinces in the 1860s about being out of sight and out of mind in Ottawa were logical and understandable. But what has grown up organically in Canada is a system of federal-provincial relations and bargaining that has nothing to do with the Senate. This largely informal system has its own problems and is in need of serious attention. I will address these issues in the next chapter.

The Senate's main function remains to review, so far as it is able, legislation passed by the senior partner in parliament, the House of Commons. The Senate's approval is required before new legislation goes to the Governor General for Royal Assent. It also picks up on current issues and holds committee meetings to explore them. But because the Senate's role in Parliament is ambiguous to say the least, these hearings and their reports, however worthy, receive little attention.

Discussion of Senate reform began only five years after Confederation, in 1872, and it has bobbed along near the surface of Canadian political life ever since. The first major reform was in 1927, when the British Judicial Committee of the Privy Council in London, which was then Canada's highest court of appeal, decided that women were "qualified persons" and entitled to be appointed members of the Senate. These appointments were for life until the second major amendment in 1965 requiring Senators to retire at age 75. Discussion of Senate reform intensified in the 1970s, and in the last fifty years there have been about thirty major proposals for fundamental changes, all of which have failed to get traction. In the 1980s, Western alienation, stemming largely from Ottawa's energy policies, spurred a campaign for Senate reform based on what was known as the "Triple-E" template. This envisaged Senators being elected, with equal numbers from each province, and having effective power to force the House of Commons to review or drop programs the Senate believed harmed the national interest. This proposal was seen in central Canada as an effort by Alberta and the other Western provinces to circumnavigate or nullify Ottawa's National Energy Policy.

Making constitutional changes that affect general principles in response to a particular political confrontation or crisis is never a good idea. Triple-E failed, but in 1987 the Alberta government enacted legislation allowing for the election in the province of candidates for the Senate. The legislation and the elections, however, were not binding on the prime minister in his choice of appointments. Stephen Harper had been an advocate for an elected Senate, and when he became prime minister in 2006, he began trying to change the practice so that prime ministers were required to accept the elected provincial candidates.

A scandal over the expenses of some Senators in 2013 gave Harper an opening to push his reform agenda. But before putting forward legislation, Harper asked the Supreme Court for its opinion on the constitutional implications of what he proposed. Harper wanted to know whether parliament alone could amend the constitution to enact new term limits for senators, to allow direct elections, and even to abolish the Senate entirely. Harper's move attracted a great deal of attention, and all ten provincial governments, as well as the administrations of the territories intervened in the case. The Supreme Court ruled that Harper could not ask parliament alone to do most of what he was proposing. Fundamental changes to the Senate invoked the Constitution's amending formula, the court decided, and therefore needed substantial provincial agreement. The court did, however, say there were some minor aspects of Senate reform that were purely political in nature, and not changes to the Constitution, that the federal government could change unilaterally.

With no national consensus on whether Senate reform was necessary, how its members were chosen, what their function should be, and whether the Upper House was even necessary, the whole issue died. There was a return of interest in 2015 when the new Prime Minister, Justin Trudeau, built on his 2014 decision to expel all Liberal Senators from the party and require them to sit as independents, a move allowed by the Supreme Court ruling. He pledged to "create a new non-partisan, merit-based process" to advise on Senate appointments. This he did, and the Independent Advisory Board for Senate Appointments is made up of three permanent federal members and two members from each of the provinces or territories when a vacancy is to be filled. As is evident from its name, the board is advisory and its recommendations to the prime minister are not binding. The political scientist and historian, Donald Savoie, was a member of the board for New Brunswick, and reported that the process worked as intended. There was no outside interference. All Canadians were free to apply for a Senate post. The board's deliberations were free and fair. If there was a bias, Savoie wrote, it was against putting forward the names of former politicians. The board submitted five names to the prime minister and he chose from among them.

Since then, Trudeau appears to have abandoned his good intentions. As I write this in late 2023, there are fourteen vacancies in the 105-seat Senate. It is as though the Prime Minister can't be bothered with the Upper House and considers its sober second thoughts on his legislative agenda to be irrelevant. If so, Senators seem to feel the same way. Attendance by Senators for debates and votes in the Upper House has become deplorable. A story published by *The Globe and Mail* in March 2023 showed that on the 104 Senate sitting days since November 2021, an average of twenty-five members — nearly a quarter of the population of the Upper House — didn't show up for votes on the passage of legislative bills or other matters of Senate responsibility. Of the nineteen votes on legislation in the previous five months from when the story was published, twelve votes were attended by fifty-eight senators or fewer. This lax work ethic does not appear to be giving Canadian taxpayers value for the Senate's $126.7 million-dollar budget for 2023 – 24, an increase of 70% since 2015 when Justin Trudeau's government came to office. Maybe some senators are earning their $164,500-a-year salaries, which come with a tax-free housing allowance to keep a pad in Ottawa, and a generous pension, but many are not.

Thus in its present guise the Senate looks to be a waste of time and money. It is nothing much more than a comfortable sinecure for political waifs and strays. There are good and strong arguments that Canada does not need a Senate. The task of sober second thought on the work of the House of Commons is well and good, but it is only of value if the senators have legitimacy in their roles, and there is little willingness to give them that. Yet, once the old and now irrelevant notion of regional representatives in Ottawa is chucked out, there is important work that a reformed and legitimate Senate could do.

Canada's Parliament and politics in general need sober primary thought far more than they do sober second thought.

Our governments don't put nearly enough thought into the long-term implications and repercussions of the decisions they make. One of the most serious defects of modern democratic parliaments is their short-term thinking. They seldom, if ever, look beyond the next election up to five years down the road. Most of what they do — the legislation they pass, the policies they adopt — is viewed through the lens of how the voting public will respond come the next election. Short-termism is democracy's big weakness and it offers great opportunities to competing, well-established autocracies, such as the People's Republic of China, where the ruling Chinese Communist Party forms policies based on the implications of its actions in a generation's time — twenty years — and often more.

Beijing seldom looks for instant gratification. It looks down the road and calculates that while the result of its actions today may seem inconsequential or even negative, the long-term payoff will be significant. A good example of this mentality is the thirty-year program Beijing followed to take control of the South China Sea, which carries over 30% of global maritime trade. This was accomplished by dozens of minor advances starting with the jokey declaration in the early 1990s of a Chinese municipal government for the South China Sea. Then, using its maritime militia made up of China's massive fishing fleet, Beijing challenged the territorial claims of other littoral states such as Vietnam, the Philippines, and Malaysia, sometimes with violence. Beijing could and did deny it controlled or directed the fishing fleet militia, even though the ships' captains were trained how to manage confrontations at sea by the People's Liberation Army Navy. The United States (the only nation competent to respond effectively) never judged these maritime skirmishes as serious enough to warrant an aggressive push-back. It was only when Beijing began building seven artificial islands in the sea and constructing military bases and airfields that Washington began to pay serious attention, but by then the game was over. The result is that Beijing is now in a position to control whatever happens in one of the world's busiest seaways.

Beijing applies this long-range mindset to its economic and diplomatic forays. The culture of functioning on a twenty or thirty-year calendar gives Beijing a huge advantage, for example, when it makes investment agreements with countries and companies embedded in the culture of short-term gains. The Belt and Road Initiative of Chinese Communist Party boss and China's President Xi Jinping is a typical piece of thinking beyond the time horizon. This massive, expensive plan for transport and communications infrastructure investment that would create a network with China at its hub is nothing short of a blueprint for the People's Republic to become the world's predominant superpower. At the moment, the plan has been put into hibernation after a decade of frenetic activity as countries in its path have become suspicious of its implications. But in all likelihood, Beijing is waiting until memories fade.

All too often decision-making in democracies is accompanied by short memories and narrow visions of communal and national long-term interests. This is a particular weakness in Canada, where so many of the considerations of our national interests and national security, for example, have been left to allied powers; Britain in the first half of this country's life and the United States since the Second World War. The contrast with our cousins, the Australians, makes the point. They too are an immigrant country working with British-manufactured institutions, and doing it with a small population on a vast landmass. The difference is that Australians have had to take responsibility for their own security as they carved out their individual place in the world. They have had a clear-sighted idea of what they needed to do and how they could achieve it. Unlike in Canada, this has become a largely bipartisan effort. Changes of government in Australia do not mean 180-degree swings in foreign or defence policy as they frequently do in Canada.

It would be very beneficial to introduce into Canada's daily political discourse voices and opinions giving a view of the long-term implications of what the House of Commons is doing. And those voices should have some political legitimacy; not enough to overrule the House of Commons, which must remain supreme, but well-founded enough so that they cannot be brushed aside without consideration.

To give just one example: The COVID-19 pandemic and the disruption in the international supply chain of goods and services it triggered, exposed all kinds of weaknesses in the Canadian economy stemming from the actions or inactions of past governments. The 1984 privatization by the government of Prime Minister Brian Mulroney of the Connaught Laboratories is a good example. From its founding in 1914, this institution played a singular role in the advancement of public health in Canada. The laboratory's sale in 1984 was propelled by the ideological belief that government should not be in business, forgetting that the business of public health has been a government responsibility since the founding of the first cities seven thousand years ago. Connaught Laboratories were a world class and world famous developer and supplier of vaccines; it was not long after its privatization that foreign medical and pharmaceutical companies came sniffing at the door. For the first few years the federal government, on occasion chivvied by the governments of Ontario and Québec, blocked foreign acquisition of Connaught Labs, citing national interest. But in 1989 Mulroney allowed ideology to outweigh common sense and he approved the sale of the company to the French Institut Mérieux, which moved Connaught's capacities off shore. Thus, when COVID struck in early 2020, Canada discovered that it no longer had the ability to develop or manufacture vaccines quickly to meet the needs of the public.

It was already known in 1984 that the world was entering an age of pandemics: cheap air transport and mass tourism facilitated the spread of disease. The first tourist-borne pandemic, HIV-AIDS, was already making itself known. Mulroney was warned about the long-term implications of the Connaught sale, but this was framed as a political attack from the opposition and was easy for him to ignore. It might have been more difficult for him to sell Connaught, and in the end saved many Canadian lives, if the warnings had come from a body with both political legitimacy and expertise at looking into the future implications of current political decisions.

Another good example of short-term decision-making having long-term implications was the disbanding of the National Ports Police in 1997 by the Liberal government of Jean Chrétien. This specialist force of 100 officers policed Canada's six major ports. Its purpose was to detect and stop smuggling rackets of drugs, guns, and stolen goods such as cars. The Ports Police were replaced by private security guards, municipal police, and local detachments of the Royal Canadian Mounted Police. None of these replacements, however, have the special dedication to policing the ports that are necessary to be successful. Moreover, early in 2000, it was found that most of the Ports Police's most sensitive intelligence files on corruption, smuggling, and infiltration by organized criminal gangs disappeared at the time of the force's disbandment and were never passed on to the new units. The short-sightedness of the move was evident from the beginning and there have been numerous calls over the years, including by a Senate committee, for the Ports Police to be re-established. The result is that organized crime gangs operate almost un-challenged in Canada's ports.

Last year, six tons of Canadian-produced methamphet-amine was intercepted leaving the Port of Vancouver for Australia and New Zealand. An investigation by Postmedia crime reporter Kim Bolan published early in 2024 showed that groups like Hells Angels are working closely with Mex-ican crime cartels, Asian organized crime gangs, and Middle Eastern groups to traffic drugs and stolen goods from Canada, especially cars and trucks.

We have a historical example of institutionalized long-term policy-making on which to draw. The Haudenosaunee people of present-day southern Ontario and Québec, and the northeast of the United States, and better known in English and French as the Iroquois, have what they call the "Seventh Generation Principle." This concept, one that has been traced back as a theme of Haudenosaunee government to the twelfth century CE, requires decision-makers to envisage the impact of what they do today on their successors living in seven generations' time. With shorter life spans at that time, the principle envisaged trying to look forward about one century. In ages when economic and social changes were slow, that was feasible. Thinking forward seven generations these days is impossible. Experts can't even agree what the population of the Earth is likely to be in 2050 and whether it will be growing or shrinking. But in very many fields of human life, the people most closely involved can make an intelligent stab at imagining how today's actions will affect what happens twenty years down the road.

To this end, I have a suggestion for an elected Senate that could still be a chamber of sober second thought, but which would also be charged with examining and commenting on the future implications of today's actions by the House of Commons. The Senate could thus become guardian of the Seventh Generation Principle. Mine is not a definitive suggestion. I can see several holes in it, and problems that would need to be addressed and overcome to make it function.

I had been wondering how one could put together a Senate of futurologists who had the experience and expertise to comment on the present and future impacts of actions taken by the House of Commons. At the same time, these people needed to be elected from clearly defined elements of society, but not to the degree that their political legitimacy challenged that of the House of Commons. It came to me that I had seen a legislature that might fit the bill during my time as Asia Correspondent for *Southam News* when I lived in Hong Kong in the years running up to the British colony's return to Chinese sovereignty in 1997. The British never allowed full democracy in Hong Kong, but they did create an elected legislature with some power and the political legitimacy to give strong advice to the governor and his executive council. The core membership of the legislature was made up of people elected by what are called functional constituencies.

These, at the time of the 1997 handover, were twenty-eight sectors of Hong Kong society ranging from economic and professional groups, such as real estate developers and lawyers, to social welfare organizations and representatives of sports and the arts. In all twenty-eight cases, everyone working in an enterprise, from the janitor to the boss, got to vote on who should represent them in the legislature. The attraction of this system for the British was that it brought into the government process a body of expertise from the Hong Kong community with some political legitimacy, but not enough to challenge the authority of the governor appointed by London.

Creating a Canadian Senate on a similar model could create an institution with an individual view of the world that would enhance the work of the House of Commons. Canada could create as many functional constituencies as it took to adequately represent all aspects of society, and they could elect representatives to the Senate on a different timeline from that of the House of Commons. A ten-year term might make sense. The functional constituencies could be encouraged to adopt and elect candidates with deep experience in their particular sectors, and with the ability to judge the effects of government regulations and actions taken by the House of Commons. As in Hong Kong, the functional constituencies would include professional, economic, and social institutions, but some thought and fine tuning would have to be done to ensure geographic balance in the make-up of a Senate elected on this basis. Canadian institutions tend to have their headquarters in central Canada. There would also have to be provisions so that both Canada's official languages were represented. To fulfill the obligations of geography and language it might be necessary to elect two members from each functional constituency.

A side benefit of a Senate based on functional constituencies is that it might put a dent in Ottawa's booming lobbying industry. There are now about 5,000 registered lobbyists in Ottawa, taking money to bend the ear of MPs and ministers on behalf of people and organizations that want something from government. Even when well regulated, lobbying can never quite pass the smell test, and the Canadian version has produced a regular stream of scandals. So why not give the sort of people and organizations who hire lobbyists the chance to get elected to a reformed Senate and win a platform to set out the interests of their niche in our society; their functional constituency? If they have useful arguments to make, let them make them in public and take responsibility for what they say.

CHAPTER FOUR

The Constitution:
Nine Decades of Dithering

CANADIANS, AND ESPECIALLY Canadian political leaders, are sometimes and on some issues a nation of ditherers. Avoiding making decisions or taking responsibility for questions that need to be addressed has become a fixture in the national character partly because of the curse of geography. History has put us next door to and intertwined with the world's dominant economic, cultural, and military power. That means that there are many aspects of Canadian life over which we have little or no control even if we wanted more. There is no clearer picture of that reality than looking at the country with which we share sibling DNA, Australia. Australians have a responsibility to manage their national and security interests in a way we don't and never have. Australians are not ditherers. They can't afford to be.

Geography aside, within Canada the dithering gene has been implanted in us because of the way the country was put together. Canada is a federation constructed from building blocks designed for a unitary state. But it is not a unitary state and never could be. It is a federation with a plethora of levels of government, usually with overlapping duties and obligations. This creates confusion about who is responsible for what, and thus a wonderful opportunity for political leaders to avoid taking responsibility. Sometimes the dithering is simply because political leaders can't be bothered. Responsibility is easy to avoid, and someone else at some other level of government will do what's needed. Sometimes dithering is strategic. The system provides easy outlets for political leaders who don't want to do something that might damage their popularity. I will deal later on with some recent examples of the perils of the dithering syndrome for Canadian democracy and political life, but in order to try to find some way out of the vicious circle of passing the buck, it is necessary to understand how this national characteristic came into being.

Canada is one of the oldest of the world's very few continuous democracies. It was in March 1848 that Canada, then made up of today's Ontario and Québec, achieved responsible and largely representative government with the backing of London and its Governor General, Lord Elgin. The democracy with the most males on the voters' lists established in Canada 176 years ago even outstripped the franchise in Britain at the time and was well ahead of the slave-owning government by moneyed elites in the United States. Lord Elgin and London were responding to a democratic movement that had grown out of rebellions in 1837 and 1838 in Upper and Lower Canada demanding political reform. This outbreak of popular unrest prompted the union of the two colonies in 1840 as an attempt to create a functional administration. But Canada was still ruled by London's Governor General aided by an appointed executive council heavily influenced by the robber baron oligarchs. It was not good enough, and the 1840s saw the growth of a pro-democracy movement led by young political activists Louis-Hippolyte LaFontaine of Montreal, and his friend and political ally, Robert Baldwin from Toronto. It was the original alliance of English and French-speaking Canadians, and if anyone deserves to be called the fathers of Canadian democracy it is these two.

On March 11, 1848, Lord Elgin invited the two to form a government. The LaFontaine-Baldwin administration introduced and enacted in a remarkably short period an extraordinary amount of foundational legislation on which our parliamentary democracy still stands. They passed laws to encourage immigration, to promote transportation, to create public schools and universities, to establish an independent judiciary, create a professional civil service, and set the rules for democratic municipal affairs. Meanwhile, similar drives towards responsible parliamentary government were going forward in Britain's Atlantic colonies of Nova Scotia, New Brunswick, and Prince Edward Island.

The 1850s were a time of difficult external pressure on Britain's remaining North American colonies. Some of those pressures came from Britain itself. The repeal of the Corn Laws in response to demands from free trader merchants and capitalists ended tariffs on grains from outside the British Empire, and thus ended preferential markets for Canadian farmers. And the British public and establishment were growing agitated at the increasing and seemingly endless cost of maintaining their empire. They wanted the colonies to take more financial and political responsibility for their own lives, but, for the time being, under the guiding hand of London.

At the same time, there was a head of steam building in the south. There was economic pressure from the United States as the industrial revolution that had begun in Britain after the Napoleonic wars at the start of the century took hold in North America. Then there were a multitude of issues for the Canadian and Atlantic colonies spilling out of the American civil war in the mid-1860s. The US had a strong expansionist gene in its DNA. There was real and well-founded fear that after its victory over the southern states, the Union Army would turn north and gobble up Britain's remaining North American colonies. And if not all of them, then certainly the largely undeveloped and minimally governed western lands all the way to British Columbia. This period saw a number of border disputes, and also raids into Canada by Fenians — supporters of Irish independence who expected, mistakenly, that Catholics in what are now Ontario and Québec would join them in rising up against British rule. The security of Britain's remaining North American possessions seemed tentative at best.

Several political leaders in the Atlantic colonies thought that their economic and physical insecurity could be minimized by creating their own union, similar to the union of Canada East and Canada West. In September 1864, representatives from Nova Scotia, New Brunswick, and Prince Edward Island met in Charlottetown to discuss this idea. The meeting was gatecrashed by the leaders of the Canadian union, Sir John A Macdonald and George Etienne Cartier, laden with crates of champagne. Their aim was to take control of the Maritime colonies' union talks and impose their own agenda. The union of the two Canadas was not going well. There was political deadlock and, in essence, no functioning government.

Macdonald and Cartier believed a wider union, a greater Canada, was the answer to not only their own problems, but for the future of British North America all the way to the Pacific Ocean. They hijacked the conference and for a week pummelled the Maritimers with arguments for a union based on loyalty to Britain, and a strong central government with provinces having control only over local affairs. The national parliament would have two houses. Members of the House of Commons would be elected on the basis of constituencies of roughly equal population. But the upper house, the Senate, would have an equal number of members from each province whose responsibility would be to represent the interests of their province, and to apply sober second thought to legislation passed by the House of Commons.

Macdonald wanted a unitary state with an entirely dominant central government based on majority support in the House of Commons, and with the Senate and Governor General providing only marginal restraint. But there was a good deal of suspicion of Macdonald's agenda in the Atlantic colonies and Québec. Macdonald eventually recognized that he was not going to get his way and that a form of federation had to be cobbled together. This framework was set out in seventy-two resolutions approved the following month, October 1864, at a conference in Québec City charged with setting out the terms of confederation.

Those resolutions reek of reluctance on all sides. There was no substantial vision of trying to create a nation of distinct character and purpose, molded to fit the environment it inhabited. There were only copies of transplanted British institutions whittled into shape to fit the Canadian template.

There was no amending formula. Virtually all the powers of the day went to the federal government. Very little was done to make national institutions sensitive to the individual needs and circumstances of the provinces and regions. And, of course, it never occurred to the Fathers of Confederation to include First Peoples in the negotiations on Canada's creation. That loose end was tied off in 1876 with the enactment of the Indian Act, a paternalistic and offensive document the purpose of which was to strip Indigenous peoples of their languages and cultures, and promote their assimilation as quickly as possible. Women had no direct role either, other than overseeing the food, drink, and entertainment of the delegates. Married women only got the right to own property in 1859, five years before the Québec conference, and they still had to get their husband's permission to sell that property. Canadian women got the right to vote in federal elections in May 1918.

The irony is that the powers that were handed off to the provinces such as education, health, language, and the direction of municipal government, were minor matters at the time. But in the century-and-a-half since, these have become the main responsibilities of government, affecting the daily lives of most Canadians. The dominance of the provincial governments in the lives of Canadians has created a minefield of regional imperatives and clashing cultures into which Ottawa steps gingerly. Now and then federal governments have intruded on provincial responsibilities to try to establish national standards, or to bring a national perspective to common problems, such as a public health emergency or a housing crisis; but, all too often, this simply provides a stage for one provincial government or another to dramatize its outrage at the intrusion, or to be deliberately obstructive. Cunning provincial leaders lurk in the long grass, let other provinces wrestle with Ottawa, and then grab every dollar they can from the federal treasury. Federal governments are not innocent in these exchanges. If there are political points to be gained for the ruling party in Ottawa by displaying the provincial leaders as a bunch of squabbling brats clambering over one another to grab tax dollars, it will do so.

The political historian Richard French has said, with some justification, that "the political culture of Canada may be defined as a profound sense of regional grievance married to a discourse of entitlement." What he means is that very many Canadians feel hard done by in the confederation deal and are certain that someone else in some other part of the country is benefitting more than they do. French notes that nearly three quarters of Canadians feel their province gets back less in federal spending than the taxes they send to Ottawa. And nearly three quarters of Canadians feel the federal government favours one region of Canada over the others, and very few feel that they live in the favoured region.

Some writers point to the fact that the Fathers of Confederation were a rough-and-ready crew when explaining why the original Canadian constitution, enshrined by the British Parliament in 1867 as the British North America Act, is such a dog's breakfast of leftovers and unappetizing peelings. They have noted that of the thirty-three delegates at the Québec Conference, only one was a university graduate. The rest had functional educations, but could not be called erudite. There is a clear contrast with the American Founding Fathers, almost all of whom were university trained classicists who had thought and argued deeply over all aspects of democracy in ancient Greece, the social and political theories of the Enlightenment, and the implications of the French Revolution.

My judgement is that Canada, despite all the flaws in its founding, got the better deal for two main reasons. The first is that however grand the intellect and the vision of the US Founding Fathers, they were on the wrong track in creating a constitutional republic, which might or might not be a democracy as well. As it turns out, the US has been a fully functioning democracy for only a decade or so in the 1970s during its nearly 250 years of existence. Annual rankings usually put the US well into the section on "flawed democracies" and around 30th on the global list of representative and responsible governments.

Canada from the start had the benefit of the parliamentary system, which is a vastly superior approach to democracy than those based on a written constitution subject to interpretation by lawyers and judges. When it is working properly, parliamentary democracy, with its emphasis on the supremacy of the direct representatives of citizens in the House of Commons, is far more adaptable and able to absorb punishment than constitutional systems.

That leads to my second view, which is that the adaptable and pragmatic Canadian Fathers of Confederation were far more suited to the task of making things work, even if they didn't fit very well, than the American would-be Athenians. The Americans were trussed and hobbled by what was intended to be the perfectly worded guide to the creation of the "shining city on the hill." They still are manacled by their constitution and have not worked out what and for whom their country exists.

Canada's political curse has been that confederation by force of circumstance tried to blend parliamentary and constitutional approaches to democracy. These two facets of Canadian federalism were always destined to clash, but it took 120 years for this pressure to come to a head. Because the delegates at Québec City could not agree on a formula to amend or change the British North America Act, this document, Canada's constitution, remained a piece of British legislation under the authority of the British parliament. So, until the constitution was finally patriated in 1982, all changes to the Canadian federal-provincial partnership had to be made in London, and all legal challenges decided by British courts.

There were nineteen amendments to the British North America Act after the creation of Canada in 1867 and patriation in 1982. All deal in one way or another with federal-provincial relations and the division of powers. Some deal with the creation of new provinces Manitoba, British Columbia, Saskatchewan, Alberta, and Newfoundland. Other amendments set out such things as provincial rights over natural resources on federally controlled lands, and adjustments to the formula for distributing among the newer provinces new seats in the House of Commons. In 1949, Britain gave Ottawa greater power to amend the constitution without having to go cap-in-hand to London, but by that time the British political establishment was keen to get rid of its remaining colonial ties to Canada.

The sacrifices made in the First World War by the largely self-governing Dominions — Canada, Australia, New Zealand, South Africa, the Irish Free State, and Newfoundland

— led to widespread public feelings in those countries that they had earned the right to end Britain's remaining control over their affairs. London agreed, and a report by Arthur Balfour in 1926 said that Britain and the Dominions should be constitutionally "equal in status." This led to the British parliament passing the Statute of Westminster in December 1931. This codified the Balfour Declaration and gave the Dominions the right to take into their own hands all the powers over their countries still held by the British parliament. Other Dominions accepted the offer and made off with London's gift. Canada did not. The federal and provincial governments could not agree on a formula for making future changes to the Canadian constitution. They asked London to hang on to this power to amend the Canadian Constitution until Canadians could come up with their own way of doing it. Well, stuff happens. Attention gets diverted. First there was the Great Depression of the 1930s and then the Second World War. Then there was rebuilding and the post-war expansion of Canada as new immigrants poured into the country.

That wave of immigration, with many from countries that had no historic link with Britain, blended with Canadian domestic politics to arouse dormant interest in the constitution. The Quiet Revolution in Québec in the 1960s, and the not-so-quiet birth of a strong independence movement in that province raised questions about Canada's continued constitutional links to Britain and the Monarchy. Canada's centenary in 1967 also had a significant influence on the public mood and opinion. Was it not time, after a hundred years of official nationhood, for Canada to take full control of its constitution?

These sentiments led to the federal Minister of Justice, E. Davie Fulton, and his Québec counterpart, Guy Favreau, to push for agreement on an amending formula that would allow patriation of the constitution. After polling the provincial premiers, they came up with a relatively simple proposal.

All provinces would have to approve amendments relevant to provincial jurisdiction, including the use of the French and English languages. Only the affected provinces would be needed to approve amendments concerned with a particular region of Canada. Two-thirds of the provinces representing half of the population, as well as the federal Parliament, would be needed for amendments dealing with education.

Ironically, considering Favreau's involvement, it was Québec Premier Jean Lesage who scuppered this effort. He argued that the formula would not allow Québec and French Canada to fully develop their potential within Canada. Without the support of Québec this effort at patriation was doomed.

After Pierre Trudeau took over the leadership of the Liberal Party from Lester Pearson and became Prime Minister in 1968, he took up the challenge and put some serious effort into getting an agreement with the provinces that would allow for patriation of the constitution. A federal-provincial meeting in 1971 came up with the Victoria Charter. The amending formula in this document played with the Fulton-Favreau template of majority agreement across Canada for changes, but added the stipulation that Ottawa, Ontario, and Québec should have a veto over whatever was proposed. This was a backhanded way of acceding to Québec's demand for a veto. The issue became less divisive if it was diluted by giving Ontario and the federal government the same privilege. Then British Columbia insisted that it deserved a veto too. And despite being given a veto, Québec Premier Robert Bourassa wasn't happy either. He wanted Ottawa to give full control over social policies to the provinces, and to give them the money to pay for the programs. Trudeau refused, and Bourassa withdrew his support for the charter.

It was at the Victoria conference that Trudeau played his opening gambit on a new entrenchment of Canadians' rights. The Conservative government of John Diefenbaker had enacted a Canadian Bill of Rights in 1960. This covered all the usual civic rights such as freedom of speech, equality before the law, and political rights. The bill is still in force, but its problem then and now is that it only applies to federal jurisdictions. Trudeau wanted a legal entrenchment of rights that was universal across Canada and applied to all the country's institutions.

Trudeau made several other attempts in the 1970s to get agreement on an amending formula, but without success. The 1980 referendum in Québec on independence fixed the nation's attention. During the federal intervention in the campaign, Trudeau made unequivocal promises about constitutional protection for the French language across Canada, and that he would act unilaterally to patriate the constitution with these provisions if the premiers did not agree to a patriation package. When the independence referendum was defeated, Trudeau felt his intervention had been the deciding factor. With that came a responsibility to press ahead towards patriation, even without the agreement of the provinces. So the "people's package" he proposed sending to Westminster included a Charter of Rights and Freedoms attached to the constitution, and not a bill of rights under the jurisdiction of Parliament. That was a fateful decision that continues to generate aftershocks to this day.

In addition to keeping his promise to French-speaking Canadians to put the guarantee of their language rights beyond the reach of politicians, Trudeau made another argument for a charter of rights embedded in the constitution. He said that the bulk of immigrants to Canada came and would continue to come from countries with no parliamentary heritage, and who therefore had little or no understanding of how their rights as Canadian citizens would be protected and ensured. I was among many who did not understand or share that argument. It seems very reasonable that people taking up citizenship in a country with a political and social culture that is unfamiliar should go to the trouble of finding out how their new home works rather than expecting the country to adapt to them.

More troubling is that the Charter of Rights and Freedoms comes from a concept of constitutional democracy with written rules and boundaries that are in fundamental conflict with the agility and responsiveness of a well-tuned parliamentary democracy. It is a well-tested truth that elasticity and inventiveness always win. Rigidity always loses.

The government of Margaret Thatcher and the British Parliament were quietly appalled and some of their members very angry at Trudeau's expectation that they would give unquestioning agreement to passing a bill opposed by most of the provinces and including a written constitution with a charter of rights. British parliamentarians understand the oil-and-water relationship of constitutional and parliamentary democracy. The British government and all the parliamentary parties told Trudeau as plainly as they could that his bill would not pass unless it had majority support from the provinces. In September 1981 the Canadian Supreme Court ruled that while Trudeau had the legal authority to make a unilateral application to Britain for patriation of the constitution, he shouldn't do so. A convention had grown up, the judges said, that such an important constitutional development must have "substantial" provincial support.

In November, Trudeau returned to the table with the premiers. It was a hot and heavy few days that finally won agreement from all the provinces except Québec. The agreed amending formula said that any changes to Canada's division of powers would require support from the Parliament in Ottawa, the Senate, and at least seven provinces representing over half the Canadian population. On the Charter of Rights and Freedoms, some of the provinces dug in their toes. They demanded that there be an opt-out clause so that they could sideline charter rights that they considered detrimental to the interests of their province. This became Article 33 of the Constitution, known as the "notwithstanding clause." Trudeau agreed reluctantly, but insisted in response that Ottawa retain powers of "disallowance" of any such provincial moves if the federal government considered a provincial opt-out on rights to be unacceptable.

The Canada Bill passed through the British Parliament and on April 17, 1982 and was proclaimed by the Queen in Ottawa. That, forty years later, is where things have stuck. Worse than that, to a significant degree they have gone backwards. The inclusion of the Charter of Rights and Freedoms has distorted Canada's parliamentary democracy by inserting the courts into the equation of people's rights and liberties. The provinces have now found a way to routinely skirt elements in the Charter they don't like. They have taken to including references to the notwithstanding clause in any legislation that might be appealed to the Supreme Court in order to forestall adverse judgements. Ottawa could use its own power of disallowance to impede the provinces' short circuiting of the Charter. But that would set a constitutional crisis in motion, and no federal or provincial government has been willing to do that yet.

There is something else about that period in the late 1980s and early 1990s that is important. This was a time of unusual disruption in Canadian politics. To an outsider looking at postwar Canada, the country looked like a collection of one-party states. Ontario had been a Progressive Conservative principality since the Second World War. Alberta had been Tory since Peter Lougheed beat the long-established Social Credit government in 1971. Saskatchewan had elected New Democratic Party governments, and its precursor, the Cooperative Commonwealth Federation, since the Second World War. Manitoba had been Progressive Conservative country since the early 1950s. British Columbia had its own exotic political habits. For four decades from 1952, with only one short break in the early 1970s, voters elected governments from the Social Credit party, a socially and economically conservative movement that began by peddling some peculiar ideas on monetary and fiscal reform. The Atlantic provinces were more variable, and Québec was not concerned so much about a party's name as its nationalist credentials.

All those loyalties, however, were usually reserved for provincial politics. Some, like Alberta, voted Conservative in both federal and provincial elections, but a skill enjoyed by many Canadians was to keep both their federal and provincial leaders slightly off balance by voting for opposing parties in national and provincial elections. Ontario voters in particular were masters of this game. While consistently sending Conservative governments to Queen's Park for two generations, Ontario voters were equally responsible for repeatedly electing Liberal governments in Ottawa. Those habits were shattered in the mid-1980s and onwards. That upheaval, with its change of characters and provincial positions on the constitution, is an essential element in what happened when Brian Mulroney tried to tie off the loose ends after patriation.

Pierre Trudeau didn't think there were any loose ends. In his memoirs, he wrote that he was not happy that Québec had not signed on to the patriation package, nor was he happy with the package he had been forced to accept, especially the notwithstanding clause. But he saw no reason for anyone to touch the Constitution for a generation or more. Brian Mulroney, who led the Conservatives to power with a majority government in 1984, thought otherwise. He had won a crashing victory with 211 seats in the 282-seat House of Commons, and a key reason for that success was winning 58 of the 75 seats in Québec. This was a once-in-a-lifetime victory in Québec for the Tories. Mulroney had the advantage of being a Québec native from Baie-Comeau and he had a high public profile as a politically active, well-connected lawyer. He also, during the campaign, promised to find a way of allowing the Québec government to accept the 1982 Constitution "with honour and enthusiasm."

That purpose appeared to get a boost in 1985 when

Québec voters ousted the sovereigntist Parti Québécois and elected provincial Liberals led by Robert Bourassa. In his campaign, Bourassa set out his five conditions for signing on the Constitution. These were: recognition of Québec as a distinct society, giving the province a veto on constitutional matters, requiring an input from the Québec government on the appointment of Supreme Court justices, giving Québec an embedded role in the federal preserve of immigration, and limiting federal spending powers. Mulroney got on well with Bourassa and chose to see the five conditions as a shopping list that could open negotiations. At an Edmonton meeting with all ten premiers in 1986, Mulroney agreed to consider constitutional reform with Bourassa's five conditions as a starting point.

The eleven first ministers, without officials or advisers in the room, met at Wilson House on the shores of Meech Lake in the Gatineau Hills, in April 1987. Mulroney fancied himself the master of this kind of stagecraft, this kind of comradely salesmanship that nudged everyone into agreeing to his agenda. After nine hours of discussions, Mulroney announced they had reached consensus on Bourassa's five requirements, plus a compromise agreement that new senators would be appointed from lists provided by the provinces until a full-blown reform of the Upper House could be negotiated. The main change to Bourassa's five demands was that they were expanded to include all provinces. Thus all provinces were to be given powers over national immigration policy. All provinces could claim cash from Ottawa if they chose to opt out of federal programs. The appointment of senators and Supreme Court judges would be drawn from names provided by the provinces.

Mulroney's Meech Lake Accord was not greeted with joy in the streets. Early polls did show that most Canadians supported the agreement, but that quickly changed as the public started hearing from people involved in political and constitutional matters who were shocked and horrified at what Mulroney had done. Pierre Trudeau led the charge against the Meech Lake Accord. In an article published in English and French language newspapers, Trudeau wrote that the accord seriously altered the balance of federal-provincial authority in Canada in favour of the provinces to the extent that it could be disastrous for the survival of the country. He called Mulroney a "weakling," and the premiers "snivelers" forever begging Ottawa for aid.

Trudeau's intervention had a dramatic effect. Many groups took a second look at the accord, and joined Trudeau in expressing powerful objections. Women's groups, some ethnic communities, and the main First People's organizations all voiced strong opposition to the aggrandizement of provincial power envisaged in the accord. These objections provoked second thoughts among the premiers and the federal parties. Both Manitoba's NDP Premier Howard Pawley and Ontario's Liberal Premier David Peterson were faced with revolts by their backbenchers and recanted on the accord. They wanted the issue of provincial powers reopened. But Mulroney and the other eight premiers responded to Trudeau's attacks by doubling down. Even so, they tweaked the wording on the "distinct society" clause for Québec and tightened the language dealing with federal spending powers. Pawley and Peterson were pulled into line and all eleven leaders signed the accord on June 3, 1987. Mulroney declared that Québec was once again part of confederation. There was a standing ovation.

Criticism of the accord continued and intensified. There were many hard words said about the secretive nature of the process Mulroney orchestrated, and the exclusion of many people and organizations that had a legitimate interest in any adjustments to the constitution. There was also bitter commentary on the special status offered to Québec as a "distinct society." Some felt that this created an imbalance within confederation, while others feared the accord's provisions would lead to the decline and perhaps eradication of English-speaking communities within Québec and of francophone communities in the rest of Canada. Others, such as women's groups and First People's organizations, were concerned that Québec was being offered the power to overrule the provisions of the Charter of Rights and Freedoms. In the West and Atlantic Canada, the premiers withdrew their support for the accord when faced with public and political dissatisfaction that more had not been done to reform the Senate and ensure it was a voice in Ottawa for provincial interests.

Because it would change the Constitution's amending formula, adoption of the Meech Lake Accord required the agreement of the federal and provincial legislatures within a three-year timeline. This meant that June 22, 1990, was the last day the accord could be approved. Québec, Saskatchewan, and Alberta all ratified the accord in 1987. But even while these legislatures were debating the matter, the accord was effectively killed in New Brunswick. The government of Conservative Premier Richard Hatfield was defeated by the Liberals led by Frank McKenna in the October elections of

1987. McKenna had a list of changes he wanted made to the accord, especially protections for New Brunswick's status as the country's only officially bilingual province. An election in Manitoba in April 1988 produced a minority and unstable Conservative government, politically unable to support the accord. A change of government in Newfoundland in 1989 brought Liberal opponents of the accord, led by Clyde Wells, to power.

There was a lot of shuttle diplomacy and bargaining in 1989 as various attempts were made to find compromises that might save the Meech Lake Accord. When June 1990 rolled around, Mulroney thought there was hope of saving his baby. He invited the premiers to Ottawa. They met for a week in the Government Conference Centre with the media in the room, which meant playing to the cameras. Mulroney tried to unleash an atmosphere of high drama by proclaiming that the survival of Canada as a nation depended on the premiers accepting the accord. The dissident premiers bowed to the pressure and agreed to accept the accord, but with reservations. These reservations were that Meech Lake should be a preliminary accord, and there must be guarantees of future federal-provincial conferences to sort out matters such as Senate reform and issues of concern to Indigenous peoples.

After a week of talks and with some hesitation and misgivings, the premiers signed the reworked accord. Mulroney might have secured a solid, if debatable spot in Canadian constitutional history at that point if he had kept his mouth shut. But strategic silence was not a Mulroney skill. He couldn't stop himself from telling two reporters from *The Globe and Mail* that he had intentionally scheduled the meeting for the last days before the deadline when the accord must be approved in order to put maximum pressure on the premiers. Predictably, this admission that they had been gamed outraged several of the premiers, though by that time they had had enough dealings with Mulroney to know the way he operated. It was his public admission that was most insulting. The upshot was that the terms of the Meech Lake Accord were not put before the Manitoba and Newfoundland legislatures for approval before the June 22 deadline. In Manitoba, the accord didn't even come up for debate. One member of the legislature, Elijah Harper, refused to give the unanimous consent necessary for there to be an emergency debate on the accord. The Meech Lake Accord was dead, but not so the problem of Canada's dysfunctional constitution.

Those problems landed most heavily on the head of Robert Bourassa in Québec. The failure of the federal-provincial negotiations to recognize Québec as a distinct society and embed protection of its language and culture in the Constitution inevitably sparked renewed support for the sovereignty movement. Bourassa found it necessary to promise that he would hold a referendum in 1992 asking whether Quebeckers wanted either a new constitutional agreement with Canada or sovereignty for Québec.

Mulroney assigned his predecessor as Tory leader, the Minister of Constitutional Affairs, Joe Clark, to start negotiations with the nine non-Québec premiers on a new constitutional accord. Meanwhile, Clark negotiated with the Québec Premier through a back channel that required messages being passed via a third party. This cumbersome process was surrounded by a swarm of conferences and discussion groups.

Mulroney had been stung by the secrecy of his Meech Lake Accord initiative, so he opted for excessive openness on his second try. Two panels were appointed in Québec to explore the constitutional possibilities and two more nationally. The federal government then held five national conferences to explore proposals. These led to a report by the federal government that became the basis for negotiations between Ottawa and the provincial and territorial governments. Meanwhile, the Assembly of First Nations, the Congress of Aboriginal Peoples, the Inuit Tapirisat of Canada, and the Metis National Council were also drawn in to the talks. All this was brought to Charlottetown in August 1992.

The Charlottetown agenda had five principal items, though running through them all was an effort to encourage Québec to sign on to the 1982 Constitution. This was diplomatically masked, nowhere more obviously than in what was called the "Canada Clause." This was intended to be one of those humble-but-proud moments when Canada demurely set out its national values. Chief among these, of course, was recognition of Québec as a distinct society within Canada. Along with this went the declaration of Canada as a federated parliamentary democracy respecting the rule of law.

The declaration voiced support for official language minorities everywhere in the country, applauded racial diversity, supported gender equality, and the equality and rights of the provinces as distinct regions within Canada. The Canada Clause set out support for the Indigenous peoples of Canada and their rights. This was an introduction to another of the five sections on the agenda dealing in greater detail with Indigenous communities. This section proposed a major step forward in changing the relationship between Canada and First Peoples, even though, as in the past, Indigenous leaders were not invited to the discussions about their future. The Canada Clause would have enshrined in the Constitution the right to self-government for First Peoples. This would have given Indigenous communities their own order of government that was autonomous from both the federal and provincial levels. This may have looked like putting Indigenous governments on an equal footing with their federal and provincial counterparts, but there was a kicker in the small print. First Peoples' laws would have to meet Canadian standards of "peace, order, and good government," and they would be subject to the Charter of Rights and Freedoms. This meant that the ultimate authority over Indigenous governments and their activities would be the Supreme Court. This would have made it difficult for some Indigenous communities to re-introduce traditional forms of government. Canadian values would continue to be imposed, but from behind a screen of self-government.

The Charlottetown meeting attempted to deal with some long-standing federal-provincial disputes over jurisdictions and the division of power. The outline gave the provinces much greater authority over natural resources, mining, forestry, and cultural affairs while giving Ottawa responsibility for only national cultural institutions such as the Canadian Broadcasting Corporation and the National Film Board.

The accord also tackled the always contentious issue of taxation and government spending. The Constitution from the start had given Ottawa much greater taxation authority than it had the provinces. But Canada's development as a social democratic country led to the provincial government responsibilities — such as healthcare, social services, and higher education — costing far more than provinces were able to fund. Over the years, federal governments had agreed to make transfer payments to the provinces needing help to finance their social responsibilities, but these transfers came with conditions. The money had to be spent in ways Ottawa found acceptable. Any attempts to tinker with universal access to healthcare, for example, would attract a penalty from Ottawa. The Charlottetown Accord would have gone a long way to remove the heavy hand of Ottawa. The accord said that as long as the provincial programs met national standards, they would get the money.

There were also some significant changes to Canada's governing institutions in the accord. The main one was to adopt the demands from Western Canada for a "Triple-E" Senate, that is an upper chamber that was equal, elected, and effective. Each province would have the same number of senators, and they would be elected either directly by voters or by members of the provincial legislatures. There were also proposals to eliminate barriers to the free flow of goods, services, labour, and capital within Canada.

The popularity of the Mulroney government was at low ebb at the time, and the Canadian public was in a cynical mood about the Charlottetown Accord, remembering the opaque process of the Meech Lake Accord five years before. Mulroney decided that the Charlottetown Accord would be put to a national referendum, though he had little choice because Alberta, British Columbia, and Québec had laws in place requiring referendums on constitutional amendments.

Having a direct public say in those three provinces and not anywhere would have been the kiss of death to the accord, though the shadow of rejection hung over it from the start. This was surprising, because it was a pretty good deal, certainly better than the Meech Lake Accord. But its negative reception spoke about the churlish mood of Canadian voters in their attitude towards the establishment in general and the government of Brian Mulroney in particular.

The referendum was framed to need a majority "Yes" vote in Québec and collective majority support in the remaining nine provinces. All three major national parties backed the accord, as did the leading First People's organizations, some women's groups, and business leaders. All ten provincial premiers supported the accord, and the media, by-and-large, rode the bandwagon. The main opposition, however, was potent. Pierre Trudeau roused himself from retirement as he had at the time of Meech Lake. He announced that the Charlottetown agreement would mean the end of Canada as a nation because, in his view, it would cause the disintegration of the federal government by giving far too much of Ottawa's authority away to the provinces. For those who were disinclined to follow Trudeau's lead, a new voice from the political right came out of Western Canada. The leader of the Reform Party, Preston Manning, argued that the proposed Senate reform didn't go far enough. He also opposed guaranteeing Québec 25% of the seats in the House of Commons, and the idea of recognizing Québec as a distinct society. Predictably, the Bloc Québécois's Lucien Bouchard and the Parti Québécois's Jacques Parizeau damned the accord because it didn't, in their view, give Québec enough power.

These opponents caught the truculent mood of the Canadian voters. When the ballots were counted after the October 26 vote in 1992, a majority of 54.3% of eligible Canadians had voted against the accord on a voter turnout of 71.8%. Nearly 46% of voters supported the accord. This apparently close outcome hid some important detail. Only in New Brunswick, Newfoundland, Prince Edward Island, and the Northwest Territories did a majority of voters support the accord, and they did so by substantial margins. Everywhere else it was soundly defeated, except in Ontario, with only 50.1% support.

Since then, federal leaders have made it a virtue not to touch the constitution. That said, in 2006 the House of Commons did pass a motion recognizing francophone Quebeckers as a distinct nation within a united Canada. Oddly perhaps, the one attempt to reopen the constitution in an effort to resolve its divisions came from Québec. Liberal Premier Philippe Couillard in 2017 proposed marking Canada's 150th birthday in 2017 by negotiating a deal that Québec could sign. He got short shrift from Prime Minister Justin Trudeau, who barked back: "We are not opening the Constitution."

There are indeed times when it is best to let sleeping dogs lie, and many people experienced in the trench warfare of Canadian federal-provincial relations will say firmly that opening the constitutional Pandora's Box is best avoided. Experience says that the outcomes are unpredictable and seldom good. But there are warning signs aplenty that ignoring the unfinished business of the constitution is not going to be an option for much longer. There will be no safety in dithering, and it is going to be essential to take control of events before events take control of themselves.

CHAPTER FIVE

The End of the Supremacy of Parliament

ONCE PIERRE TRUDEAU in 1981 agreed to the inclusion of Article 33 (the "notwithstanding clause") into the constitution package, much of the rationale for the Charter of Rights and Freedoms evaporated. Trudeau's central argument for embedding the Charter in the Constitution was to ensure that Canadians' rights applied in every province and territory. The existing Bill of Rights, brought in by the government of John Diefenbaker in 1960, did not do this. It only applied to the federal government and its legislation. It was not a very effective document, perhaps because of its limitations. As a result, governments in the 1960s and 1970s seldom tried to expand its provisions despite major changes in and expansions of societal views in that period about human rights that should be protected. Trudeau wanted to ensure that the full panoply of human and civic rights in Canada applied right across the country and that there would be no provincial enclaves where they did not apply. Coming out of his campaign to defeat the 1980 referendum in Québec on "sovereignty association," a euphemism for independence, Trudeau was determined to enshrine in the Charter official language rights for French throughout the country. Trudeau, too, was a constitutional democrat by instinct, and not a natural supporter of parliamentary democracy.

At the tactical level, Trudeau saw the campaign in Canada and London to "patriate" the constitution from the British Parliament as an opportunity to pull an end run on the provinces. By including the Charter of Rights and Freedoms in the patriation package he could avoid endless debate on its contents. Indeed, his original plan had been to avoid debate altogether by making a unilateral request by Ottawa to London, based on the belief that he did not need provincial support. Then London would do the dirty work of sending back to Canada the amended Constitution with the Charter attached. The British government and parliament were already unhappy with what Trudeau was asking them to do, knowing they were being played for suckers. Things went wrong when Canada's Supreme Court ruled at the end of 1981 that while Ottawa could legally make a unilateral request to London, the convention had grown up over more than a century of Canadian confederation that there should be "significant" provincial support. The court did not put a number on how many supporting provinces were sufficient.

The Supreme Court ruling forced Trudeau to rethink and go back to the negotiating table in search of significant provincial support for his "People's Package." But to get this, Trudeau was forced to accept the proposal from Alberta Premier Peter Lougheed to include Article 33, the notwithstanding clause, in the Charter of Rights and Freedoms. The clause gave the provinces and the federal government the ability to opt out for five years from one or more of the rights and freedoms in the Charter that were standing in the way of legislation. After five years, the objection could be renewed — ad infinitum.

Behind Lougheed's pushing for Article 33 was a belief shared by many of his provincial colleagues that the Charter of Rights and Freedoms was going to change the nature of Canadian parliamentary democracy at both the federal and provincial levels. This would happen because the Charter, and its applications and interpretations, were not in the hands of Parliament or the legislatures, but in those of the justices of the Supreme Court of Canada. Those judges were and are appointed, they are not accountable to anyone, and they have their own view of the world that comes in through the small and narrow window of their sequestered lives. Lougheed's aim with Article 33 was to subject the Charter to some parliamentary oversight, as inadequate as it might be. Trudeau agreed only very reluctantly and got the premiers' verbal agreement that the notwithstanding clause was to be used only *in extremis*; very infrequently and only when there was no other option. At the same time, the federal government had the power of "disallowance," meaning that it could overrule the province and insist on adherence to the charter rights. But the convention was and is that Ottawa would use this power only when there was no other option. So far, the power of disallowance has not been used, and there would undoubtedly be a major constitutional crisis if it ever was.

This has proved to be the most damaging result of the institution of the Charter with the Supreme Court as guardian. It has diminished the role of members of parliament and members of the provincial legislatures because they have little to say about the views and feelings of their constituents on a variety of matters and on social issues in particular. All concerned parties know from the outset of debates and discussions on social issues that it will be the Supreme Court that decides the issue on the basis of what is written in the Charter, and not on the basis of what Canadians think and feel. Some MPs and their provincial counterparts are perfectly happy to hand difficult issues such as same-sex marriage and the wearing of religious symbols to the court. In this, they are contributing to the diminution of their own mandates as representatives of their constituents and to the belief among the public that elected members of parliament and the legislatures are people of little consequence and no power.

Once the agreement had been made to include the notwithstanding clause, there should have been some reflection about the validity of keeping the Charter of Rights and Freedoms in the Constitution package. The Charter has a much longer list of rights than the Bill of Rights, but with Article 33, these are no more secure against provincial abstentions than was Parliament's Bill from 1960. But in 1981 and 1982, the juggernaut of patriation was unstoppable. With provincial objections out of the way, apart from those of Québec, the natural instinct was to avoid complications and let the campaign run its course.

Many people saw at the time what is even more clear with forty years of hindsight. That winter of 1981 – 82 would have been a good moment to junk the Charter of Rights and Freedoms, and focus instead on strengthening and broadening the scope of the Bill of Rights. This would have kept the issue of recognized rights where it belongs, in the hands of the people's elected representatives in Parliament and the legislatures. It would also have stopped the evolution of the Supreme Court into, in effect, an appointed, unaccountable parliament on matters of social policy in Canada. In the United States there is an ongoing argument about how that country's constitution should be interpreted. Should it be seen as the Founding Fathers wrote it? Should it be viewed through the lens of how society functioned in the eighteenth century? Or should the intentions of the constitution be translated into modern times? This is a perennial problem with constitutional democracies, and an excellent example of why the more adaptable and responsive approach inherent in parliamentary democracy is preferable. The Supreme Court justices have made it clear they consider the Charter of Rights and Freedoms to be a "living tree" that grows and expands its shelter as society grows and changes. But in a parliamentary system, Supreme Court Justices are not the right people to make such decisions. The experience of the last forty years has shown that the court's interpretation of the Charter of Rights is sometimes at variance with large segments of Canadian society. The judges are working solely on their interpretation of the law, and not on the mood of mainstream Canadian society, of which they are not representative.

The friction between provincial governments and Ottawa over the Charter has been growing at an accelerating pace. Article 33 was used almost immediately by Québec in 1982. In recent years, its use by Québec has become commonplace, but has also been invoked by Saskatchewan, Alberta, and Ontario. Canada appears to be approaching a time when the article will be routinely invoked in legislation in order to forestall appeals to the Supreme Court, and rulings from the judges that overturn the aims of provincial governments.

Disputes over the Charter, the Supreme Court, and Article 33 have become a central element in the polarization of Canadian politics. Those to the right see the Charter as a left-Liberal straightjacket that was foisted on them. They see activist judges bolstering and extending the boundaries of legally protected liberalism into areas that affront their conservative social values. They see invocation of Article 33 as a legitimate right and proper way of trying to curb the instincts of the Supreme Court when they run counter to provincial values. Meanwhile, people to the left of centre in politics see the Charter as an embodiment of what it means to be a tolerant Canadian. From this standpoint, challenging and overriding aspects of the Charter on matters such as the right to strike or public expression of religious devotion are not only assaults on those rights, they are attacks on the Charter as a whole and a lunge at human rights in general.

It takes little insight to understand that Canada is approaching a constitutional crisis flowing from these increasingly frequent clashes over the Charter. And perhaps this country needs a constitutional crisis. What we have at the moment is not fit for purpose and it will be even less useful in our fast-changing world. But the decisions made in crisis are seldom solid and long-lasting. It is worthwhile now, before that inevitable crisis arrives, to take the time to examine what has happened with the four decades of the Charter of Rights and Freedoms and to consider how to address its defects.

The Charter of Rights and Freedoms made the Supreme Court into a third chamber of Parliament, but as a rogue player, which, unlike the other elements in our system, is not accountable, is totally independent, and whose decisions cannot be directly challenged. The court alone decides what it considers important. It decides it will hear some cases and not others. It interferes in the workings of both the federal and provincial governments without responsibility for how its rulings are to be implemented. The internal debates and discussions of the nine judges are kept secret for at least fifty years. It is the very epitome of despotic and unaccountable authority that parliamentary democracy is designed to overcome. As the assertive and activist judges of the Supreme Court have imposed themselves on national and provincial policy-making, they have diminished the role of both Parliament and the legislatures. With that, of course, has come the erosion of the role and importance of the citizens' elected representatives. The public's confidence in their MPs and provincial and territorial legislative representatives has shrunk rapidly since the introduction of the Charter of Rights and Freedoms in 1982. This is for the very simple reason that as the authority of the Court and its power to interpret social policy has ballooned, so has the role of our elected representatives withered. And yet Canadians have allowed, and some have even applauded, the injection of this destructive body into our system.

The intrusion of the Supreme Court on the political stage over the last forty years has prompted several suggestions on how to shine the light of public scrutiny on how justices are selected and how they operate. There are proposals that the process of picking Supreme Court judges be more open and transparent; more like the American system, including ratification of the appointments by Parliament. Also, in the interests of openness and accountability, some suggestion that judges be required to be more open about how and why they reach their decisions, and that there be more public accountability for their actions. The calls for transparency are aimed not only at the Supreme Court judges, but also bodies like the Canadian Judicial Council, which considers disciplinary action against federally appointed judges.

There was a case that fed this clamour in 2023 arising from the opacity around the story of the resignation from the Supreme Court of Justice Russell Brown. On January 28th that year, Justice Brown spoke at a judicial gala at a hotel near Phoenix, Arizona. The next day, a complaint was made against him to the Canadian Judicial Council. Three days later Justice Brown was placed on leave from the Supreme Court by Chief Justice Richard Wagner. What had happened at the hotel was never made public by any of the judicial authorities. It was made known that at the end of March, the Judicial Council appointed a panel to review the incident and decide whether what happened was "serious enough to warrant removal of the judge." The panel was about to table its report in June when Justice Brown resigned. He had been given forewarning of what the report said. But as he was no longer a judge, it was decided not to release the report at all.

It was left to a newspaper, *Vancouver Sun*, to ferret out what had happened in Phoenix. Justice Brown was alleged to have harassed two women, and to have had an altercation with a man. The police were called but no charges were laid. After his resignation, Justice Brown issued a statement complaining against the process and said he had clear evidence disproving the claims made against him. This was the first time since the Judicial Council was created in 1971 that one of its inquiries could have led to the removal of a Supreme Court justice. An editorial in *The Globe and Mail* said Canadians deserve to know what happened. "The loss of a Supreme Court justice should not end in a swirl of uncertainty," the editorial said. "Trust cannot be taken for granted and needs to be earned. Transparency is the remedy."

I think it is highly desirable that there be more openness about the inner workings of the Supreme Court and greater accountability for the actions of the judges. But I am opposed to any changes in the selection and appointment process that would have the effect of giving the Supreme Court added political legitimacy. This would inevitably be at the expense of Parliament, and would cement in place the court's position as part of the legislative process. I am opposed to anything that undermines the supremacy of Parliament and, indeed, the legislatures, as the forums where the representatives of Canadian citizens who elected them make decisions about the life of the country.

Canadian judges used to know their position in the structure of our public life, and that was not to interfere in the workings of the elected Parliament and legislatures. After Canada created the Supreme Court in 1875, it was not a busy institution. Donald Savoie writes in his 2019 book *Democracy in Canada* that,

> Canada's courts were careful to preserve parliamentary supremacy for a century. The courts did not go beyond deciding how the constitution distributed power between the federal and provincial governments. When it came to

government officials exceeding their authority, "the remedy
was seen to be with parliament, not the courts."

Numerous legal scholars and academic experts on public administration have catalogued a wealth of examples of
how the Charter of Rights and Freedoms in the hands of the
Supreme Court has on many occasions usurped the role of
Parliament and the legislatures. Supporters of the charter and
the court can and do argue that these have allowed recognition of social changes like same-sex marriage and medically
assisted suicide when Parliament might have been unwilling
to do so. It is true that Parliament, using the old Bill of Rights,
would likely have been much slower and more cognisant of
the attitude of mainstream Canada before approving such
amendments. We all must decide whether hastened rulings
on these and other important social issues have been worth
the erosion of democracy, now that the power has been taken
away from Parliament.

At the end of 2014, in a cheeky nose-thumbing, the Macdonald Laurier Institute, a right-of-centre policy organization
based in Ottawa, gave its annual "Policy-Maker of the Year"
award to the Supreme Court of Canada. The report setting
out the reasons for the award looked at ten judgements over
the course of the year that had in effect written national policy
that the government could not directly challenge. Summaris-
ing the award, the Institute wrote:

> In the last year, the Court has effectively taken Senate
> reform off the federal agenda for the foreseeable future,
> torpedoed both the governing Conservatives' reform

program and the Opposition New Democrats' policy to abolish the Senate. The Court has struck down much of Canada's prostitution legislation, resulting in a dramatic rewriting of the law by the current government. It has changed the landscape in parts of Canada for Aboriginal rights, affected tools available for fighting crime and terrorism, and cast into question how future appointments to the Court from Quebec will be managed. One would be hard-pressed to find another actor in Canada who has had a greater impact on such a wide range of issues than the Court has had last year, such that the moniker Policy-Maker of the Year is appropriate. The Court, no doubt, would resist such a label on the view that it simply applies the law as part of its constitutional mandate. But the policy impact of its recent decisions is clear.

One of the habits of the Supreme Court, which provincial governments especially find particularly annoying, is to pronounce on citizens' rights and demand that they be respected without taking any responsibility for how that should be done. Often these rulings effectively dictate to provincial governments how they should manage their affairs, but again without offering any helpful advice on how. A well-known example of this last habit comes from New Brunswick in 2008. The provincial government decided reluctantly to cancel its early French immersion program for financial reasons. This was a difficult decision in Canada's only formally bilingual province. Some parents took the issue to court, claiming their Charter rights were being violated. Interestingly, the Court denied that claim. Their Charter rights had not been violated, the Court said. But then the Court went on to say that the Education Minister had not allowed enough time for debate on the issue. The time the minister had allowed for consideration of the change was "unfair and unreasonable," and for that reason alone the court upheld the parents' claim. The court's decision was based not on legal precedents, but simply on how the province managed the affair. New Brunswick decided not to appeal, and instead opened a new round of public consultations before introducing a slightly revised cutback in the early French immersion program.

Another example of judicial overreach occurred in 2012. The Supreme Court decided unanimously that school boards in British Columbia did not have the right to avoid providing programs for special needs children because of budget constraints. Justice Rosalie Abella wrote, "Adequate special education is not a dispensable luxury. For those with severe learning disabilities, it is the ramp that provides access to the statutory commitment to education made to all children in British Columbia." While one can applaud these sentiments, one can be alarmed at an unaccountable court taking the authority to decide who in times of need has to make sacrifices and who does not. In a parliamentary system that's a judgement to be made by the elected legislators.

Savoie, the Canada Research Chair in public administration and governance at the Université de Moncton, has commented even more forcefully. "It is not possible to overstate the impact the Charter of Rights and Freedoms had on Canadian politics," he wrote in 2019. "The notion that Parliament is supreme now belongs to the history books." I believe Savoie is right. But I haven't any realistic idea how the Charter of Rights and Freedoms could be removed and Parliament's Bill of Rights regain its position as the dominant document on this matter, and I have seen no serious ideas from anyone else. It may be, however, that a work-around will be achieved by pre-emptive use of the notwithstanding clause by the provinces. This is the direction in which the provinces are heading by their ever more frequent invocation of Article 33 in legislation. If that is coupled with intense efforts to restore the supremacy of Parliament and the legislatures as the country's law-making institutions, the result might be the sidelining of the Supreme Court as the third chamber of Parliament.

CHAPTER SIX

Canada:
The Unconsummated Marriage

AFTER THE DEBACLE of the failed Meech Lake Accord in 1990, ideas quickly started being thrown around about how to keep the Canadian federation afloat without a constitution supported by all the provinces. Canadians are sometimes very good at attacking objects by indirection. That is, after realizing they can't successfully attack a castle by the front gate, they head off over the horizon and then suddenly appear at the unguarded back door. Joe Clark, Brian Mulroney's Minister of Constitutional Affairs and point man on arranging a follow-up to Meech Lake at Charlottetown, tried this approach. In preparing agenda items for the planned First Ministers Conference at Charlottetown in 1992, Clark snuck in among the twenty-eight items an idea that came from one of the more interesting and turbulent characters in the whole constitutional soap opera.

Mel Smith, a lawyer, joined the British Columbia civil service and became the chief advisor on the constitution to four provincial governments from 1967 to 1987. In the

1990s, after he had retired from government, he became a multimedia personality on all things flowing from the constitutional impasse. One of his ideas was to create a Council of the Federation, a sort of King Arthur's round table including the Prime Minister, the ten premiers and the leaders of the territories. Smith's idea, picked up and espoused by Clark, was to make this council an established part of the Canadian legislative system. It would have the power to vote on proposed federal legislation affecting the economic union of the country. It would have been able to make decisions on federal spending for new Canada-wide programs where the cost was shared with the provinces. To be approved, decisions by the Council of the Federation would need the support of the federal government and seven provinces representing at least half the population of Canada.

The insertion of a new level of government into an already overcrowded field of governing authorities with which Canadians had to deal was greeted with outrage. Most Canadians already had to contend with at least three and often four levels of government ranging from federal through provincial, and often a regional authority, before arriving at their local municipality. All of these have their hands in the pockets of the taxpayers. Sticking another level of government between Ottawa and the provinces did not go down well. Smith responded boldly, saying the Council of the Federation would not add more bureaucracy or need more money. It would only give constitutional authority to people who were already doing the work covered by his proposal.

There was truth in that view, but few people were convinced, and Clark expressed surprise at the vehement reaction.

He said it was clear there was no consensus and the federal government would have to take that idea off the Charlottetown agenda. It did, but the idea of a Council of the Federation did not die. It morphed into something else. We do have a Council of the Federation today. It usually meets twice a year, but its members are only the premiers and territorial leaders. Neither the Prime Minister nor any of his ministers are members. It has very high-flying objectives of promoting "constructive Confederation" and influencing the national Parliament and government's agenda on current issues. It has had considerable success in influencing Ottawa, but there is still no formal relationship with the federal government.

It became evident to our forefathers early on in the story of Canada that the Senate was never going to be an effective forum for discussing and resolving relations between Ottawa and the provinces. Wilfrid Laurier first grasped this nettle and in 1906 called a meeting with the premiers to discuss the perennial issue of financial subsidies to the provinces. The meeting was called at the request of the provinces, which had already set up their own network at meetings among themselves in 1887 and 1902. The provincial network was formalized in 1960 at the instigation of Québec's premier, Jean Lesage. What was called the Annual Premiers' Conference was a low-key affair, more of a summer party, barbecue, and golf match than a political bargaining or strategy session. Indeed, the main aim of the gathering was to allow premiers — and their spouses, who were also invited — to get to know each other so that they could communicate easily and honestly. The meetings received little media coverage because they were held in private, and most reporters and commentators didn't see a story beyond cataloguing the wine, beer, burgers, and resort accommodation paid for with public money.

It was after the defeat of the Charlottetown Accord, and the return to power in 1993 of the Liberals under Jean Chrétien — who had no interest in reopening the constitutional debate — that the Council of the Federation began to evolve into something more pertinent. In 1994 the Québec Liberal Premier Daniel Johnson suggested turning the Annual Premiers' Conference from a golf-game-with-burgers into something more serious; something more strategic in the relationship between the provinces and Ottawa. That idea was put on hold between 1994 and 2003 when the Parti Québécois held power in Québec. But in 2001 the Québec Liberals, then in opposition, released a report recommending what amounted to a diluted version of Mel Smith's Council of the Federation. It would have included the Prime Minister with the premiers, and territorial leaders. It was hesitant about powers of decisions-making. It offered vetoes on council decisions to the federal government, Ontario, Québec, British Columbia, and the prairie provinces and the Atlantic provinces as groups. The report envisaged that if experience warranted, the Council of the Federation would become a new level of government, much as Smith saw it.

That didn't happen. When the Québec Liberals returned to power in 2003 with Jean Charest at the helm, he had more modest ideas. Even so, what he proposed was a formal, regular gathering of political leaders to discuss federal-provincial issues even though the Prime Minister was not a member. Their objectives, set out in their founding agreement in December 2003, are:

1. Strengthening interprovincial-territorial cooperation, forging closer ties between the members and contributing to the evolution of the Canadian federation.
2. Exercising leadership on national issues of importance to provinces and territories and in improving federal-provincial-territorial relations.
3. Promoting relations between government which are based on respect for the constitution and recognition of the diversity within the federation.
4. Working with the greatest respect for transparency and better communication with Canadians.

All noble stuff, and the Council of the Federation has a reasonable track record of influencing the federal government's agenda. A report in 2018 by the Institute for Research on Public Policy found that of 108 identifiable calls for action made by the council, nearly two-thirds (sixty-six) had been at least partially addressed by the federal government. Among those, twenty-nine were judged as having been fully addressed by Ottawa. These included engaging in free trade negotiations with Asian countries, streamlining federal-provincial environmental assessments, establishing a national housing strategy, improving marine safety, and increasing funding for health services. The report concludes "Overall, CoF appears at least moderately successful at gaining the attention of the federal government when it comes to acknowledging or taking action on provincial/territorial priorities."

Yet the Council of the Federation remains only a lobby group. A top-of-the-line lobby group to be sure, because its members have their own political legitimacy, but still only a lobby group. It can probably never be more than that. There are two main reasons for this. One has been the inability of the premiers to agree to common stances on many contemporary issues that should be put to Ottawa. Often there is even basic disagreement about what the most pressing issues are. The meetings are closed, so reports are second hand via political spin doctors, but it is easy to envisage Québec seeing issues of cultural and linguistic protection as paramount, while Alberta and Saskatchewan hammer on about energy, and British Columbia expresses deep concern about climate change. One of the few questions where they have been able to form a common front is healthcare, and this always boils down to demanding more money from Ottawa without strings attached.

At the same time, a succession of prime ministers in Ottawa, starting with Jean Chrétien in the 1990s, has shown a distinct lack of interest in talking to the premiers as a group. Chrétien and Stephen Harper in particular, have much preferred to make bilateral deals with premiers when needs must rather than calling full-blown First Ministers Conferences. It's the divide-and-conquer strategy. Even Justin Trudeau — who after winning his first election in 2015, promised to make revitalizing federal-provincial relations a priority, including holding more frequent First Ministers Conferences, has preferred dealing with premiers one-on-one.

There have been seventy-five First Ministers Conferences since Laurier invited the premiers to come to chat. They have covered the nuts and bolts of what makes Canada run, but the issues have usually been concerned with adjusting who is responsible for what, and how much money Ottawa gives the provinces to provide public services. They have almost always been in private, with political aides giving quiet briefings to reporters designed to put forward the best possible interpretation of the performance of their masters and the legitimacy of their cause. The heyday of First Ministers Conferences was in the 1960s through the 1980s when the country's centenary acted as a stimulus to try to refashion the unworkable, and for most of the time absent, constitution into something functional. When that purpose came to grief at Meech Lake and Charlottetown, the attraction for prime ministers of meeting premiers en masse died too. Pierre Trudeau held eighteen First Ministers Conferences in the white heat of patriation. Brian Mulroney was not far behind with fourteen. But Chrétien held only four during his ten years in office, and only one of those this century. His successor Paul Martin went against the trend and held five during only three years in office, but Martin was too much of a traditional Liberal for his own good. Stephen Harper held only three summits with the premiers during his eight years in office. Two of those were on the economy and one on climate change.

Federal-provincial relations in the 1970s and 1980s were such a booming business that both Ottawa and the provinces constructed departments within their governments charged with managing federal-provincial relations. Most of the provinces kept offices in Ottawa for the specific purpose of aiding the management of their relationships with the federal government. Meanwhile in Ottawa, successive governments demonstrated the importance they gave to the portfolio by appointing some of the most senior and respected public servants to run the federal end of the relationship.

Upwardly mobile officials and political aides aspired to such appointments, because that was where the action was. Now, that is all in the past. The institutional muscles that drove federal-provincial relations at the leadership level have atrophied from neglect. Relations between Ottawa on one side and the provinces and territories on the other are at the most antagonistic level that they have been for at least a generation. But these are deep waters and it is unwise to characterize the whole of federal-provincial relations by, for example, the animosity evident between Justin Trudeau and Alberta Premier Danielle Smith; Saskatchewan Premier Scott Moe; or Québec Premier François Legault. Behind these strutting and grandstanding personality clashes are a vast network of officials. By some counts there are about thirty-five intergovernmental councils operating in Canada. Some involve federal, provincial, and territorial officials. Others are only for the provinces. These intergovernmental groups tend to specialize in matters like health policy or education. For the most part they are informal groups, though there are some like the Council of the Ministers of the Environment that have been given formal status and bureaucracies. The upshot is that at the workaday level of departmental bureaucrats, the business of keeping Canada running and the public service serving Canadians usually, but not always, carries on seamlessly. But this is mostly done in private and without accountability.

The informality of these relationships may be a saving grace at times when the prime minister shows little or only intermittent interest in discussing national issues with his provincial and territorial counterparts. But it highlights the weakness that in Canada, federal-provincial gatherings are aimed more at resolving disputes than they are at coordinating approaches and policies towards issues confronting all levels of government. It also supports the argument that Canada is a bureaucracy — a country run by government officials — as much as it is a democracy.

It would be important, and ought to be simple in any thoughtful society, to expand the Council of the Federation to include the prime minister and require that body to meet for a week each year. Transparency is one of the most important elements of democracy, but it would be reasonable for the reformed council to hold both public and private meetings. There is, however, a pressing reason to question whether in twenty-first-century Canada it is desirable to have a forum where only the prime minister, the premiers, and the territorial leaders meet regularly to thrash out and resolve national issues.

Canada is and always has been a nation in active evolution. Finding a recipe for functional and equitable relations between Ottawa, the provinces, and the territories has been a long and unsuccessful story, but to a significant degree, that is yesterday's news. It is being overtaken by a new circumstance, a new Canada that is going to require a new national political dispensation. It already does. According to the World Bank, in 2021 over 82% of Canadians live in towns and cities, and the proportion is set to continue rising. Nearly half of Canada's people live in the country's six largest cities; Toronto, Montréal, Vancouver, Calgary, Edmonton, and Ottawa-Gatineau. Those cities, with just under a third of the population of the entire country, produce nearly half of the country's economic activity. For all those Canadians, their municipal government has as profound an effect on their daily lives, often more, than the provincial or federal governments. Yet, it is at the municipal government level that Canada shows the greatest and most damaging democratic deficit.

The average voter turnout for municipal elections across Canada is in the low 30% range. That means that while some cities and towns manage to attract around 40% of eligible voters to the polls, very many have turnouts in the mid-to-high 20% range. That is not healthy, nor should it be acceptable. Contrast this with federal elections in which 62% of voters turned out in 2021, and provincial elections, where the average is even higher; in the mid-70% range. But several Canadian cities are now massive when compared with the other inhabited parts of the country.

The greater Toronto municipal region has a population of almost 6.4 million people, close to half the 13.5 million population of the entire province of Ontario. It's the same story in Québec where Montréal's population of 4.3 million people is half the 8.7 million people in the province. Greater Vancouver too, with 2.6 million people is approaching half the 5.4 million people in British Columbia. In Alberta, the populations of Calgary and Edmonton add up to nearly three-quarters of the population of the province. Cities like Winnipeg, Halifax, and St. John's are equally dominant in their provinces.

All indications show that this urban reality for the majority of Canadians will only intensify. The immigration policy of the current government envisions encouraging 500,000 people a year to come settle in Canada. Some, but probably very few of those people, will choose to run a homestead on Vancouver Island or take over a quarter or half section in the Prairies. The vast majority will head for the cities and towns, in large part because the skills Canada encourages — the skills that will have got them the necessary points to have their immigration approved — are urban skills.

But our cities, and especially the metropolitan cities like Toronto, Montréal, and Vancouver, face a host of social and practical problems that their political, administrative, and fiscal resources are incapable of managing. On average, twenty-two people a day in Canada die of opioid overdoses caused by contaminated street drugs. That number is just the top of a huge iceberg of contributing issues plaguing Canada's towns and cities. Housing and homelessness are prominent among those contributors, but so are mental health issues and an increasingly bitter ideological and clinical argument about how to treat people with disorders that can pose a threat to public safety.

Street crime is not only a threat to citizens, it also has a profound economic impact. In many towns and cities people are avoiding the downtowns for shopping and entertainment. Not only are customers increasingly few and far between, aggressive shoplifting has become endemic in some city centres. Business owners are moving to suburban malls. At the same time, the working-from-home legacy of the COVID-19 pandemic has cut the number of people commuting to offices, seriously affecting the clientele available to patronize cafés and restaurants. In several of Canada's cities and towns, the downtowns threaten to become wastelands.

Legally, Canada's more than 3,700 cities, towns, and other municipalities are creatures of the provinces. It is the provincial legislatures and governments that give municipal councils the power and framework for their administrations. Equally, the provinces have the power to override or dictate to the municipalities if the mood takes them. In 2018 the Ontario government of Premier Doug Ford decided that Toronto's City Council was much too big. The council had just decided to expand its numbers from forty-four to forty-seven to reflect the increasing population of the city. Ford thought otherwise and ordered the number of city councillors cut to twenty-five. The Supreme Court, when it got to have its say three years later, said this was perfectly legal. British Columbia's Premier David Eby invoked the same paternal powers in 2023 when he announced that he intended to override municipal planning rules to address the housing shortage. His government, he said, would introduce legislation allowing up to four homes to be built on traditional single-family lots for detached houses. The changes will also permit the construction of basement suites for rent in municipalities that currently forbid them. More than that, the legislation, Eby said, would provide forgivable loans matching half the cost of the renovations up to $40,000.

No wonder then, that in this subservient position, municipalities are largely absent from Canada's system of intergovernmental relations, such as it is. Municipal representatives are not invited to First Ministers meetings when they occur. They are seldom included when Ottawa, the provinces, and territories sit down together to address specific problems. Cities, towns, and other municipalities are not invited when agreements of various sorts are negotiated between the territories, the provinces, and Ottawa. Clearly, this relationship, or lack of it, is inadequate for the task of managing metropolitan cities and towns effectively. Modern issues like climate change, pandemics, addictions crises, homelessness, and policing do not fit neatly into the brackets of federal, provincial, or municipal responsibility. But without question, municipal governments are an essential partner on all these issues and many more. Local governments need to be partners in new or remodelled tripartite constitutional arrangements. Unless addressed soon, and seriously, the administrative and democratic deficit in Canada's urban areas is going to become more and more socially destabilizing.

Canada's army of almost 4,000 municipalities is not a single beast. It is a multitude of very different communal beings ranging from unincorporated settlements in rural or wilderness Canada where there is no municipal government at all, to metropolises like Toronto, Montréal, Vancouver, Calgary, Edmonton, and Ottawa-Gatineau. These six are among the twenty-one cities making up the "Big City Mayors' Caucus" in the Federation of Canadian Municipalities. It is in this core group of six metropolitan cities where most of the serious pressures lie and where it therefore makes sense to focus attention.

These Big Six are not neatly defined identities, however. Unlike other places in the North Atlantic democratic community, Canada has shied away from clearly demarcating its cities as political entities. To one degree or another, they are all a cluster of municipalities that are often required to defend their own identities and authority with vigor. This makes it difficult or impossible to make decisions for the whole region of the metropolis on issues such as roads, public transit, housing, parks and open spaces, sewage, garbage disposal, and policing. Even though in each of the Big Six there is some form of regional council, their powers and authority are usually inadequate. The amoebic nature of Canada's metropolitan governments often makes sensible planning or administration impossible. Among the Big Six, Toronto has twenty-five component communities, Montréal has an astonishing eighty-two, Greater Vancouver is made up of twenty-one municipalities, Calgary has nine, Edmonton has twenty-one, and Ottawa-Gatineau, with its much-vaunted National Capital Commission, has twelve. Several countries around the world facing the same problem have opted to give their biggest cities what amounts to provincial status. It is not a perfect answer, but it has usually improved planning and coordinated administration. All too often, however, the creation of these mega cities has not been accompanied by an expansion or entrenchment of democracy. The result is that several of the mayors of these cities have become petty despots, free of serious questioning or accountability for their actions.

In 2022, Tomas Hachard, author of much research and many reports on Canadian municipalities, wrote a comprehensive report on municipalities and intergovernmental relations in Canada for the Institute on Municipal Finance and Governance at the University of Toronto. Hachard's paper looks at the experience of other federal countries such as Germany, South Africa, Switzerland, and Brazil, and how they have incorporated municipalities into the consultation and decision-making process. None of the experiences are a perfect fit for Canada, but Hachard says that useful guidelines can be drawn from their experience. At the moment, municipalities in Canada are simply engines for the delivery of provincial government policies. Hachard puts forward four approaches to changing that relationship.

One: Municipalities — towns and cities in particular — need the capacity and internal organization to be able to participate effectively in intergovernmental relations. That means investment in quality staff at the municipal level, but also the promotion of local government associations leading, where appropriate, to bodies overseeing regional coordination on policies and their application.

Two: Some federations have laws requiring municipalities be involved in provincial policymaking, especially on matters that directly affect the local governments of cities, towns, and rural areas. Other possibilities are the creation of councils dedicated to provincial-municipal relations, or intergovernmental councils assigned to specific issues.

Three: A constant complaint by municipalities is that they are tasked by the province to perform services without receiving the financing. Provinces should be required to give municipalities the money to perform the duties assigned to them, or the power to raise taxes to cover costs beyond their current authority to raise property taxes.

These three approaches deal with relations between municipalities and the provinces. Hachard sees this as an essential prelude towards the fourth element; creation of trilateral institutions bringing the federal government into the mix. That makes sense. Measured and purposeful approaches to institutional reform, which inevitably involve cultural changes as well, are sensible. Indeed, changes in cultural attitudes are the essential first step in a revival and expansion of cooperative federalism in Canada.

CHAPTER SEVEN

The Struggle for Votes That Count

THERE HAVE BEEN many attempts at the federal and provincial levels to reform voting systems so that the outcome of elections reflects more accurately than now the way Canadians vote. Since Confederation in 1867, Canada has used the first-past-the-post (FPTP) system by which the candidate in each constituency who gets the most votes gets elected to parliament or the legislature. They don't have to receive a majority of votes cast, just more than anyone else. The virtue of this system is that it usually produces a majority government. Its strength, then, is the political stability that Winston Churchill described as an "elected dictatorship." The price of that stability is that the results of FPTP elections seldom if ever reflect the way the majority of citizens voted or the outcome they desired. I have already mentioned the 2022 elections in Ontario when Premier Doug Ford's Conservative Party won a clear majority with eighty-three seats in the 124-seat legislature, but it was an election with an exceptionally low turnout of 43.53%. Ford won a comfortable majority government with the support of just under 18% of eligible voters. At the national level, one of the most cockeyed results was in 1979 when the Conservatives, led by Joe Clarke, won only 35%

of the popular vote, but this gave them 48% of the seats in Parliament. This outcome was even more distorted because the Liberals won 40% of the popular vote, 5% more than the Conservatives. But the Liberals didn't win in the right parts of the country, or more accurately, they won by too much in the wrong parts of the country.

A persistent criticism of FPTP is that by not producing results that reflect voters' wishes, it fuels regional discord in a country characterized by regionalism. In May 2016, three prominent political actors, former New Democratic Party leader Ed Broadbent, former clerk of the Privy Council Alex Himelfarb, and former Conservative Senator Hugh Segal joined forces to write an essay, which was published in *The Globe and Mail,* that argued Canada should adopt a proportional representation (PR) voting system, not least because of the regional tensions caused by FPTP. "In a country as regionally diverse as Canada," they wrote, "the electoral system must have the capacity of enabling a government to govern effectively and the opposition's capacity to provide informed criticism. Regional representation is required for both. Our current system is seriously deficient in meeting this requirement."

Indeed it is. The political map of Canada shows large blotches of persistent support for the Liberals in the Atlantic provinces, Québec, and urban Ontario. The Conservative heartland is in rural Ontario and much of Western Canada, especially Alberta, where they often win all the seats. The battlegrounds in federal elections are relatively small; mostly competitive constituencies in the big cities and their suburbs. The country's population spread is loaded in favour of the Liberals. They can and have won majority governments without having to worry too much about what happens west of the Ontario-Manitoba border. For Conservatives, the mathematics is more complex. They need to be able to break into the Liberal fortresses in the east in order to win. That hasn't happened very often.

This map is beginning to change as more and more people — including those who were born here and those who are newcomers — choose to live in the west, especially British Columbia. The Pacific province has become a competitive region, not only between the Liberals and the Conservatives, but also the NDP. Canada is approaching a time when it will not be possible to call the outcome of an election before the votes in BC are counted.

Demographic changes will not eradicate the fundamental unfairness of the FPTP system, however. So why is there no change or reform in sight? The answer is a very simple and ugly one. Advocating for electoral change is very popular among opposition parties, who look around the House of Commons or the provincial legislatures and plainly see they have fewer seats than they deserve. But when an opposition leader manages to become prime minister or premier, with a majority unwarranted by the paucity of the party's popular vote, the enthusiasm to adopt some form of PR disappears. The speed with which power can corrupt is startling sometimes.

In 2015, Liberal leader Justin Trudeau, in opposition at the time, was in favour of PR. During the election campaign that year, he promised that if he won, that election would be the last in Canada fought under FPTP. Well, things looked different when he did win power with 54% of the seats in Parliament, but just under 40% of the popular vote.

His enthusiasm for reform dissolved very quickly. He did go through the motions of trying to be seen to keep his promise, but without any vigour. Trudeau could have held a national referendum on electoral reform, or he could have created a citizens' assembly to explore the alternatives and come up with proposals. Instead, he sent the project to a committee.

Parliamentary committees are palliative care centres for political problems or unwelcome ideas. A year after the election, the committee recommended that the government consider holding a referendum on electoral reform. The government commissioned an online survey by MyDemocracy.ca. Online surveys may improve in future, but at the moment they are notoriously inaccurate because they catch only a sector of the population. It is also fairly easy to determine the outcome by the way the questions are framed. In this case, the questions focussed on attitudes towards democratic values rather than the nitty-gritty of PR and its various alternative systems. The survey produced the opaque results that the government needed to justify ditching the project. Trudeau said that the "broad support needed among Canadians for a change of this magnitude does not exist." In February 2017, the Liberal government dropped electoral reform from the list of promises to the voters it intended to fulfill.

A vivid picture of why party leaders turn away from PR when they have won an election on the FPTP system has been given by the organization Fair Vote Canada. It applied the Single Transferrable Vote (STV) system of PR to the results of the 2021 federal election. This system envisages constituencies that elect a number of members to parliament or a legislature, and asks the voters to select the candidates in order of preference. The difference in the number of seats each party would have gained under this system in the 2021 election is remarkable.

Under the FPTP system the Conservatives won 33.7% of the popular vote, the most of any party, but that gave them only 119 seats in Parliament. The Liberals did not win a majority, but their 32.6% of the vote was enough to win 159 seats and enough, with support from the twenty-five NDP MPs, to form a reasonably secure government. Had the STV system been in place, the Conservatives would have won six more seats, 125. This would have put them ahead of the Liberals, who would have won only 121 seats, thirty-eight less than they actually did. This outcome would have put the NDP and other second-rank parties in much more potent positions. The NDP would have won fifty-nine seats instead of twenty-five, and thus been a more muscular kingmaker. The Green Party would have lost representation under this brand of PR. It would have got only one seat instead of two. The hard right wing People's Party of Canada, however, would have gone from no seats to six. This would put Canada on the same track as many European countries that have adopted PR systems and have found that it can lead to extremist parties deciding the make-up of coalitions, and even becoming part of government.

Abandoning FPTP and adopting a new electoral system at the federal level would require the prime minister to champion the move, and there is debate among lawyers whether or not it would also require an amendment to the Constitution, with all the challenges that holds. Electoral reform at the provincial level is less complex. In theory it only requires a clear sign of popular support in a referendum, but in practice it is as difficult as change at the federal level. In the first decade of this century there were strong campaigns in Québec, British Columbia, Ontario, Prince Edward Island, and New Brunswick to introduce some form of PR. They all failed.

New Brunswick led the way when the Conservative Premier, Bernard Lord, appointed a commission to look into electoral reform. The commission reported early in 2005, recommending the province adopt a PR system. Lord said he would put the suggestion to a referendum, but he was defeated in the election of September 2006 and the incoming Liberal government didn't pursue the matter further. The government of British Columbia set up a citizens' assembly on electoral reform early in 2004. It recommended adopting a PR system, which was put to voters in a referendum attached to the 2005 provincial election.

It came close to acceptance. 57% of voters backed the change, but this was short of the 60% threshold. There was another try with a referendum in May 2009, but then only 39% of voters backed the change. A citizens' assembly was formed in Ontario in 2006 and the following year it released a report recommending change to a PR system. A referendum was held in October 2007, but with the requirement that it have at least 60% support to pass. It only got 37%, and there was much criticism that the agency overseeing the referendum, Elections Ontario, had done a bad job of informing voters of what the plebiscite was about and the options available. Something similar happened in Prince Edward Island in 2005 when only 36% of voters supported the change in a referendum. There was another try in 2016, when 52% of

those who voted supported PR. But Premier Wade MacLauch-
lan said he didn't think this was strong enough support to
proceed because voter turnout was too low, only 36%. There
was a more informal approach to the issue in Québec in 2006
when a citizens' committee issued a report recommending the
adoption of PR. The government didn't respond.

The attractiveness and virtue of proportional representation depends very much on which system is adopted. Indeed,
it is very easy for governments to ensure the defeat of a referendum on PR by including in the question a model that the
voters are sure to reject. There are three established forms of
proportional representation. All three take different approaches and have different outcomes. Then there is a system that
often gets overlooked because it is a reformed version of first-
past-the-post, but which in my view deserves serious attention.

The Party List form of PR is a fairly direct and simple
structure for elections. Each political party releases a list of
its candidates. After the election, parties are allocated seats
based on the proportion of votes they are given. But exactly
who gets elected is decided by one of two main methods,
though there are about a dozen fine tunings of these approaches. Candidates can be put forward on a "closed list,"
which means that the party has already chosen the order in
which its candidates will be elected. If the list is "open," candidates are elected based on the number of votes they get.
This system, with its emphasis on voting for the party rather
than specific candidates, is popular and seventy-six countries
use it, or variants of it. This emphasis on the party usually
means that there is no direct link via constituencies or electoral districts between the voters and the members they have

elected to the parliament or national assembly. This disloca-
tion tends to make politicians into a distinct, separate, and
professional class. It is not a parliamentary system in that
it is not a representative democracy. Some countries try to
counter this division by creating electoral districts of one sort
or another. But the reality is that the first loyalty of an elected
or aspiring politician in this system is to his or her party, not
to the citizens who will or won't elect them to office.

The Party List system almost always fails to produce a
majority government and thus demands a good deal of back-
room bargaining and deal-making in order to produce a coalition able to govern. With that, of course, comes corruption
of one form or another. Sometimes creating a workable coalition can take many months, and on occasion, years. Within
Europe, both Spain and Belgium have gone without governments for extended periods because coalitions could not be
formed. After its June 2010 election, Belgium went without
a government for a year and a half — 589 days — and Spain
had no government for 314 days after its December 2015
election. In Israel, and several European countries using the
Party List method, the need to gather minor parties into coalitions gives outsized and sometimes dangerous influence to
extremist minorities. There is a defensible argument that if
Israel did not have the form of PR that gives excessive power
and influence to small minorities of nationalists and religious
fanatics, there could have been some form of political settle-
ment with the Palestinians by now.

Another PR system, Mixed-Member proportional representation, attempts to give firm district representation while
also reflecting the national support for the parties. It does this

by giving voters two ballots. On the first they pick their candidate for the local constituency on a first-past-the-post basis. On the second ballot they vote for their preferred party. So there are two groups of people in the parliaments or national assemblies. One group is those elected by constituencies. The second is people chosen by the parties to fill the seats allocated on the basis of the proportion of the national vote the party won. This system was endorsed by the Law Commission of Canada in its 2004 report recommending a move to proportional representation. Germany uses this system at both the federal and state level, and it is also used in New Zealand and South Korea. The system has several disadvantages. It produces two classes of members of parliament or the legislature. Those who were directly elected via a constituency tend to be seen to have more political legitimacy than those who got in through the party vote. This system also invites strategic voting and even gaming of the system by, for example, splitting political parties into two in order to maximize the seats that can be won in the constituency and party bits of the election.

The STV already described was used in Canada in the early part of the twentieth century. Elections for the legislatures in Manitoba and Alberta used the system from around 1920 to the mid-1950s. Winnipeg, Calgary, and, very briefly Edmonton, used the STV's multiple candidate variant for city elections until the mid-1950s, then, like the provinces, abandoning it. Before the election, the elections commission works out from the population of the constituency and the list of electors how many votes a candidate needs to get elected. If a candidate gets more than the number of votes required to secure a seat, the surplus is allocated to the voter's second choice, and so on.

Having multiple members in each constituency makes the STV system complex to manage, and it can create political disorder at the local level as elected members from rival parties compete for attention.

Maintaining citizens' confidence in the voting system is a very important part of sustaining democracy. To that end, simple is usually best. An attractive system, I think, is one that is a fairly minor improvement on the first-past-the-post method. This is called the Ranked Ballot or Alternative Vote system. Constituencies have only one elected member, but at election time voters are given ballots on which they are asked to rank the candidates in order of their preference. The aim of the election, and therefore of the political party organizers, is to get a candidate who has the support of more than half the electorate. So, if no candidate wins after everyone's first choice is counted, second choices are added, and so on until one candidate has a clear majority. This system has two associated and obvious advantages. It tends to moderate the political discourse of elections and the operations of the legislature because every candidate and party must keep in mind that they may need to be the second choice for those who support other parties. The system discourages polarization in politics. That produces the second advantage. Ranked Ballot systems do not encourage the election of extremist politicians from the left or right, or any other fundamentalist badge. The main criticism of the Ranked Ballot system is that it usually produces centrist and unexciting governments, parliaments, and national assemblies. There are worse fates.

Even if a principled prime minister did set aside partisan advantage and decide, in the interest of Canada's democratic standing, to seek agreement on some form of proportional representation, it would be a long and uncertain process. There are no rules for how to set about such a significant change at the federal level, only voluminous speculation by lawyers and politicians. What is beyond question is that adopting a new voting and electoral system will have to go through a process of unimpeachable political legitimacy and openness. That must start with a mechanism for sorting out what the question should be in the final decision. That's not a simple matter. As I have described, there are four main alternatives to FPTP and three of them have variants and sub-variants of great complexity. All four alternatives have pros and cons that need to be weighed and assessed by Canadians as widely as possible. And, to have credibility, the process must be politically neutral, otherwise there will be accusations of one party or another seeking advantage. A number of possible forums have been proposed over the years and there is experience to go on from the provinces that have sought a PR system. Ontario and British Columbia appointed citizens' assemblies. In BC this was made up of 160 people chosen at random. They met for a year and held fifty public hearings.

The House of Commons in Ottawa is divided on the issue. On February 7, 2024, it voted on a motion put forward by New Democratic Party MP Lisa Marie Barron that advocated the establishment of a national citizens' assembly to explore the options and recommend a style electoral reform. The motion was defeated by 118 votes to 102. The proposal was supported by the NDP, the Bloc Québécois, and about half the Liberals. The Conservatives and the remaining Liberals voted against the move. Most of the Liberal Cabinet did not take part in the vote. This is unlikely to be the last word on the subject.

It is easy to dismiss the idea of a citizens' assembly as the ultimate gathering of amateurs, but it has been a valued function of democracy since it was used in Athens two-and-a-half thousand years ago. Mind you, the Greeks believed in participatory democracy. Every educated and wealthy male over thirty years of age was a member of the Assembly. That's 30,000 people, of which about 5,000 attended regularly. It was no great leap for the Athenians to put together committees to debate and decide on such matters as military spending, city finances, and aspects of government organization.

Canada is a representative democracy — we elect MPs to speak for us — so participatory democracy is an alien concept and therefore raises suspicions. In recent years, however, citizens' assemblies have become more popular as a means of addressing contentious issues in a non-partisan, non-politically polarized way. They have been used to address a range of issues from the question of legalizing abortion in Ireland to how to address homelessness in Melbourne, Australia. Undoubtedly, one of the aspects that has made citizens' assemblies far more useful than in the past is that modern data gathering and sorting systems make it feasible to put together with confidence a group of people that is truly a cross section of their society.

Advertising agencies and political parties have used focus groups for decades to test their products and performance before a small group of average Canadians. A citizens' assembly is a focus group writ large and with much more profound responsibilities. In an age of highly charged, polarized politics, it makes a good deal of sense to put together a group of perhaps a hundred citizens who represent the length and breadth of Canada and ask them to advise whether this country should change its electoral system, and, if so, what options should be put to Canadians in a referendum. For, despite Canada being a representative democracy, a question as profound as the voting system should be put to a nationwide referendum. Not only that, it should be put in a referendum with a high bar for acceptance, probably 60%. Moreover, there should be a requirement for substantial voter turnout. I believe Canadians should be legally required to vote or face fines. So, turnout on a PR referendum could be close to 100%.

There are other options for the opening round of electoral reform beside a citizens' assembly. New Brunswick and Prince Edward Island established commissions with appointed members. A problem with provincial or federal commissions is that they are too institutional, too close to the bodies whose reform they are being asked to judge. They reek of the Establishment and whatever they recommend has the musty odour of an inside job.

When some of the provinces wanted public ratification for their electoral reform proposals, they held referendums. This approach to hearing directly from the public about what it thinks on an issue has been used far more frequently at the provincial level than the federal. In the history of Canada there have been only three national referendums. In September 1898 Liberal Prime Minister Wilfrid Laurier held a referendum on prohibition of the manufacture and sale of alcohol.

The result was non-binding, which was fortunate for Laurier because 51.3% voted in favour of banning alcohol, but there was only a 44% turnout. He was able to leave the matter to the provinces. In the English-speaking provinces, most voted heavily in favour of banning alcohol. In Québec, over 80% were opposed. Thus, the national average of 51.3% in favour hid a very sharp geographic and cultural division.

There was a similar split in Canada's second national referendum in 1942 when Liberal Prime Minister William Lyon Mackenzie King was badgered by the Conservative opposition into holding a referendum on conscription and overseas military service for adult men. All the English-speaking provinces voted strongly in favour, but Québec voted 72% against.

The divisions in Canada were of a different nature in 1992 when Canadians were asked to ratify the Charlottetown Accord. It failed. In all, 54.3% of voters said no, on a 71% turnout, meaning that only 38.5% of eligible voters made such an important decision. Rejection was definitive in the West, and even Ontario approved by only 50.1%.

All in all, referendums have had a troubled and uncertain history in Canada, especially if one includes the provincial experiences. And yet it is probably the only route that gives Canadian voters a clear voice on the issue of electoral reform.

The hope, of course, is that Canadians will have greater confidence in an electoral system that produces parliaments more clearly in line with the way they voted. That confidence should encourage more of them to turn out to cast their ballots at election time. There are a couple of other moves that should be considered to encourage voting. One is to follow the model from Australia and other countries that require people to vote, and to fine them if they don't. The argument for this is that democracy comes with responsibilities as well as rights, and one of them is the responsibility or obligation to vote. The argument against mandatory voting is that it runs against the logic of a democracy being a free society. Another, less muscular way of encouraging people to vote is to make elections public holidays. A few countries such as South Korea do this, but many more achieve the same end by holding elections on Sundays, thus not disrupting the work week. Australia always holds its federal elections on Saturday, and in typical Aussie fashion turns the whole affair into a party. It's become customary for friends to hold post-voting barbecues. The Australian approach is right. Democracy and the act of voting should be celebrated and marked joyfully as a high point in the political cycle.

Celebration is only justified, of course, if voters applaud the election process and accept the outcome. Canadians need change before they can raise a glass to that.

CHAPTER EIGHT

Wellbeing

BEYOND THE CORRIDORS of power in Ottawa and the provincial capitals, out in the cities, towns, villages, and wilderness-bound settlements that make up this country, a lot of Canadians are very unhappy with their lives. They have a lot to be unhappy about. For decades, the basic health of nations has been measured by one simple number: their gross domestic product (GDP). This number represents how much the country's economy grew or shrank over the course of a year.

The forecasts are that Canada's GDP will grow by only 1% in 2024 as the country clambers out of the post-COVID-19 interest rate and inflation shambles. Clearly, that doesn't tell us much about what life is going to be like in Canada in 2024, or even give us a nuanced picture of the economy. More than that, measuring GDP accurately is notoriously difficult and the components of the equation can and do change very fast. Because GDP is such an unreliable and uninformative number that fails to represent the actual state of affairs, several governments around the world have abandoned it. The Himalayan kingdom of Bhutan has famously adopted "national happiness" as an annual index of the country's wellbeing. The World Population Review also uses "happiness" as the basis for judging how countries are doing. Canada is fourteenth on the 2023 list. Ahead of us is the usual cluster of Scandinavian countries plus Luxemburg, Germany, Austria, Australia, New Zealand, and Israel, though Israel is unlikely to have a happy 2024. Other countries and international organizations have adopted approaches that are less jolly, preferring to try to measure the "wellbeing" of their societies. To reveal this motherlode of the nation's state of health, they have drawn up long lists of information about all aspects of society that must be gathered, examined, and assessed. To this end, Finland, New Zealand, Scotland, Iceland, and Wales were founder members in 2018 of the Wellbeing Economy Alliance. It is an idealistic group, stating in its objectives that:

> We envision a world where everyone has enough to live in comfort, safety, and happiness. Where all people feel secure in their basic comforts and can use their creative energies to support the flourishing of all life on this planet. Where we thrive in a restored, safe, and vibrant natural environment because we have learned to give back as much as we are given. A world where we have a voice over our collective destiny and find belonging, meaning and purpose through genuine connection to the people and planet that sustain us.

Canada joined the alliance in 2022, and several provinces and territories have followed Ottawa's example by making all aspects of "wellbeing" central to their policy making and economic planning. Until recently, a major practical problem with planning on the basis of "wellbeing" was that there was not enough of the necessary detailed information available about the state of society to make it possible. That has changed. The United Nations and the Organization for Economic Cooperation and Development (OECD), in particular, have done a lot of work on isolating and defining the information that needs to be gathered to understand the state of wellbeing of any society.

In Canada, the University of Waterloo's Faculty of Health Sciences has become the lead academic organization behind the push to understand what constitutes social wellbeing here. For close to two decades the faculty has gathered information from Statistics Canada and another 200 reliable sources in order to produce the Canadian Index of Wellbeing. As the popularity of this way of measuring a society's health widened, a number of different approaches were developed. This sometimes led to confusion as the different approaches didn't always mesh easily. Researchers and analysts have now resolved these contradictions into a list that looks at sixty-four core elements of national wellbeing. The University of Waterloo index uses this approach. The main social sectors to study are eight "domains." These are:

- Living standards
- Education
- Community vitality
- Democratic engagement
- Environment
- Healthy populations
- Leisure and culture
- Time use

Within each domain are eight subset indicators used to closely define Canada's standing in each of these aspects of daily life.

The University of Waterloo's last report on Canadian well-being was published in 2016, and thus does not take into account the effects of the COVID-19 pandemic. A 2022 report by the Population Well-being Lab at the University of Toronto, looking more narrowly at how satisfied Canadians are with their lives, found that in the years since the University of Waterloo report, happiness and the sense of wellbeing in this country have declined on all fronts.

The authors of the 2016 Wellbeing Index got a foreshadowing of this when they found that although the Canadian economy bounced back from the 2008 – 09 recession quite quickly, there was little boost to national morale. This was largely because the benefits of economic revival went mostly to a tiny minority of the country's super rich, and the Canadian economy continued to suffer from systemic problems that have plagued it since the 1980s. The index researchers found that Canadians' working lives became more precarious after the recession, and gains made before 2008 in curbing long-term unemployment disappeared. Despite some increases in family incomes, disparity increased, and more Canadians struggled with the costs of food and housing.

Predictably, one of the first things Canadians did to keep the books balanced was to cut money and time spent on leisure, arts and culture, volunteering, and vacations. Commitment to those activities dropped 9% from before the recession and was at its lowest for over two decades. What is often overlooked is how much disparity impoverishes society. People who must hold down two or more jobs just to make a living wage, and cover housing costs that suck up 50 to 80% of income, don't do much else with their lives. They don't go to concerts or the theatre. They don't go out to cafés or restaurants to meet and talk with friends or relatives. They don't go to sporting events. They don't travel, not even day trips. They don't buy newspapers or magazines. They don't give to charities. They don't have the resources to lead fulfilling lives. Not only does it diminish them — it diminishes us all. It makes Canada a lesser place. It dictates that Canada will have a dimmer future. From that point of view, it is only a mild exaggeration to say that inflation, profiteering, and an unbalanced economy are a form of cultural suicide.

Illustrative of this is that Canadians' use of their time since the 2008 – 09 recession, and again since the pandemic, has become contorted. We are spending 30% less time with our friends than we used to, and only a third of Canadians are getting enough sleep. We are talking less to our children — only twenty-five minutes a day on average. These findings in the index are backed up by a poll done by the Angus Reid Institute published in April 2023. It found that two-thirds of Canadians are cutting back on discretionary spending, a significant increase on the organization's findings a year earlier. For many Canadians — 40% — cutting discretionary spending has not been enough. The Angus Reid survey found these people are withdrawing money from savings accounts just to pay for food and housing, the basics. About 13% of respondents are having to go even further than that just to survive. They are borrowing money from friends and family. 11% said they had had to sell assets, and among those who said they were in "terrible shape" financially, 94% said they were struggling to feed their families. The child poverty rate in Canada remains unacceptable for an industrialized country. It was 13.5% in 2020. Predictably, child poverty is much, much worse among First People's communities. It is almost 30% — more than twice the national average — broken down to nearly 34% of children in rural communities and just over 25% in urban areas. All these grim numbers are underlined by the dramatic increase in the use of food banks. A report by Food Banks Canada showed that in March 2023, there were 32% more people using their facilities than in the same month the year before, and nearly 79% more than in March 2019.

Canada used to be one of the world's model countries for its equity, for the lack of disparity between the rich and the rest of Canadians. That began to change with the era of trickle-down economics, deregulation, and the beginning of globalized industrial production that started in the late 1970s and came to a head in the 1980s and 1990s. Since then, thoughtful yet hesitant taxation polices by several Canadian governments have chewed away at the edges of disparity but have done little to address the core problem. This remains a country whose inequity of wealth distribution is not only grossly unfair, it is also close to causing social upheaval. Just look at some of the recent figures. Statistics Canada's numbers for 2022 show that the wealthiest 20% of Canadian households owned over 67% of this country's net worth. Meanwhile the bottom 40% of Canadians owned only 2.8% of the country's assets. That's right. Just over fifteen million of Canada's forty million people own just 2.8% of our national assets.

Another report on disparity in 2022, done by the Paris-based World Inequality Lab, found that the top 1% of Canadians own 25% of this nation's wealth while the bottom 50% — half of Canada's forty million people — own only 5.8% of the country's assets. More than that, the top 10% own 57.7% of the country's net worth. A report published in January 2024 by the Canadian Centre for Policy Alternatives, a left-of-centre think tank, calculated that in 2022 Canada's top five highest-paid corporate chief executive officers earned $14.9 million on average. This was $600,000 more than in 2021 when they earned an average of $14.3 million. More than that, the report found that Canada's top one hundred CEOs got paid 246 times the wage of the average Canadian worker. This means that it took the CEOs just eight hours into the new year to earn as much as their average employee would make over the whole year. If these gross payouts were based on the merit and skill of the CEOs, there might be some defence for this disparity. But this is not the case. The salary portion of the remuneration of the top CEOs is around $1 million, the report says. The rest comes from what are called performance-based bonuses in cash, stock options, and the awarding of shares. Ostensibly, these added benefits are tied to the performance of the company and thus a reward for good management by the CEO. But, again, that is not the case. The CEOs get their bonuses and other benefits even when the companies are doing badly.

Another analysis, this one by Oxfam International and prepared as the organization does every year just ahead of the Davos World Economic Forum, shows that the wealthy made out like bank robbers during the COVID pandemic. Canadian billionaires, the Oxfam report says, saw their wealth grow by 51% over the course of the pandemic. And looking over the previous decade from 2023, the report found that of every $100 of wealth created in Canada over that period, $34 went to the richest 1% of the population and only $5 to the bottom 50% of Canadians.

All those numbers shout out loud and clear that the distribution of wealth and income in Canada is a desperate social problem. This disparity cannot be allowed to continue. It breeds mistrust in the political and economic underpinnings of the country, providing a platform for glib populists, like it has already in other democracies with similar problems. Unless there is greater equity, Canada is heading for serious social upheaval. One of the most persistent critics of disparity in Canada and advocates for serious reform is Frank Stronach, the founder of the international car parts manufacturer, Magna International, whose personal wealth is said to be around $3 billion. (Indeed, the current CEO of Magna, Seetarama Kotagiri, is one of Canada's highest-paid executives, earning $36 million in 2022.) In his regular newspaper columns, Stronach has argued that Canadians need an economic charter of rights to guarantee they get their fair share of the national pie. He wrote in one column that when he ran Magna, he introduced a profit-sharing system for employees. "The company's revenue increased 60% in the first year," he wrote, "100% in the second year, and then doubled again the year after that. My only regret, looking back now, is that I didn't give employees more than 10% of the annual profits. If I had done that, Magna would be even bigger and more profitable than it is today."

Stronach argues that everyone benefits if employees are given a financial stake in the company for which they work. This philosophy is the very opposite of the way most companies are run these days, which, as Stronach has said, is leading more and more people to believe that Canada's democracy does not represent their interests and that the system is rigged against them. He urges the creation of a legally enforced national regime requiring companies to distribute a portion of profits among employees. He suggests companies with between 300 and 1,000 employees be required to share 5% of profits. Companies with between 1,000 and 5,000 employees would share 10%. Businesses with 5,000 to 10,000 employees would share 15% and companies with more than 10,000 employees would be required to share 20% of their annual profits.

It's a powerful idea that could very quickly change the atmosphere around Canada's economic life. Not least of the impacts of such legislation would be to redress the balance among the four groups involved in business operations. For the last forty years, all the power in corporate enterprises has been with the shareholders and management. The employees and the customers have been treated abysmally. Companies have been run often with the twin objectives of maximizing share value and the outlandish pay and perks given senior managers. Stronach's idea would ensure that all the people involved in a business enterprise get the appropriate recompense. A useful addition would be a requirement that public companies help their employees purchase shares in the company.

As things are, Canada is discovering what the French economist Thomas Piketty set out so eloquently in his 2014 book

Capital in the Twenty-First Century. Piketty's central argument is that oligarchy is the natural state of human society. Left to itself, without democracy or the rule of law, oligarchs will take political power and ownership of the economy. We have only to look at Russia and China today as well as some of the countries in the Middle East and Africa to see the truth of Piketty's argument. Vladimir Putin in Russia and Xi Jinping in the People's Republic of China are nothing more than their country's chief oligarchs. And as Piketty points out, the whole point of human political culture is to counteract that organic drift to oligarchy.

From its earliest days, even before the founding of the first towns and cities seven thousand years ago or so, the purpose of organized human society has been the survival of the weakest. We are a compassionate, social animal. At our core, humans are anti-Darwinian. Fighting natural selection is what we do. That is the whole purpose of the communal institutions we have created, redesigned, and evolved over the last few millennia. To date, democracy is the best structure we have found for organizing human society to maintain an equitable society and ensure that its weakest members are both supported and given the opportunity to live fruitful lives.

Canada and other established democracies are currently failing miserably in that purpose. As our democratic institutions buckle under internal and external pressures, the first signs of those failures are in the increasingly desperate lives of the weakest and most vulnerable members of our society. But gross wealth disparity is only the tip of a very big and threatening iceberg. This is happening in the context of fast and accelerating changes in the way human society functions, brought about by rapid technological change and the experience of dramatic events like the recent pandemic.

We can say with some certainty that the generation of Canadians reaching adulthood in 2024 will not be able to aspire to the quality of life of their parents and grandparents. The single-family home set in a large garden, the job-for-life with perks and benefits, dependable and easily accessible healthcare, a well-crafted education system to advance the family's children, and all of it supported by a robust national economy — these are all things of the past. Yet at the same time, from what can already be seen, young Canadians do not appear to aspire to the same things as their parents and grandparents. Many young Canadians have a very different idea from their forebears about what makes a fulfilling life. Their view of an appropriate balance between work and personal aspirations and activities, and what constitutes a sustainable economy and society may fit the direction in which Canada is going. But, before that transition is complete, we must overcome a big hump to restore equanimity to our political, economic, and social conventions that are seriously out of balance.

In the wake of the 2008 – 09 recession, the Wellbeing Index found that fewer people were working more than fifty hours in a week, and more people were working flexible hours. But the downside was and is that jobs are more precarious. One-in-three workers don't have regular work hours. One-in-twenty Canadians are working less than thirty hours a week, and not by choice. They'd like to work more, if only they could. Some chain stores are limiting the number of hours an employee is allowed to work to ensure they don't reach the threshold where the company would be required to provide pensions and other perks.

Another report, this one by accountants H&R Block and published in March 2023, found that 28% of the population, or about 8.75 million Canadians, are taking extra jobs in the informal gig economy to try to pay their way. The gig economy relies heavily on temporary and part-time positions filled by independent contractors and freelancers rather than full-time permanent employees. The work can range from driving for Uber or delivering food, to writing code, or contributing articles for online publications. In three-quarters of these cases, the people told the survey authors their gig economy jobs were side hustles because their regular jobs didn't pay a living wage. The study found that 85% of Canadians are concerned that their incomes are not keeping pace with the cost of living.

Despite the insecurity of the work market, job hopping has become the norm. A study by a group called Thinkopolis found that over half of Canadian workers stay in a job for less than two years. By analyzing the work histories of seven million Canadians, the study found that people who graduated from university in 1992 — Gen Xers — worked in an average of 3.2 jobs in the first twelve years of their careers. But ten years later, the cohort that graduated in 2002 — Generation Y — held 3.9 jobs over their first twelve years in the work force. Extrapolating from these trends, the study predicted that Canadians now in the early years of their working lives can expect to have around fifteen jobs over the course of their lives. And the prospect is that none of these jobs will be secure or will include benefits such as extended health insurance or pensions.

Another factor in this first domain of the wellbeing index is housing. It is extraordinary that in Canada in 2023 homelessness as well as inadequate and unsafe housing are major problems across the country for those living on minimum wages and young people just striding out into the world. Statistics Canada reckons that over the course of a year, upwards of 235,000 Canadians become homeless, usually for a short period of time. Still, on any one night there are 35,000 people sleeping on the streets, in parks, or in shelters across the country. As housing costs — especially rents — continue to rise, a growing number of people living on the streets have full-time jobs, but they don't get paid enough to for proper accommodation, or enough food. Among the homeless is a core of people who for various reasons are living long-term on the streets or in city parks. Often it is because they can't work because of ill health, disabilities, mental illness, or addictions. Canadian society, torn often by good intentions, doesn't seem to know how best to address these people. Institutions that used to offer grim and uncharitable options for people experiencing homelessness were closed three decades ago, and no functional system replaced them. The effects on the mood, attractiveness, and safety of Canada's major cities and some towns have been profound. Several provinces and municipalities are beginning to create new forms of institutional living that will be both empathetic and effective.

Even for those without afflictions that prevent them from getting housing, finding and keeping a home is a fraught business. A fundamental problem is that in our struggle to attain financial security, the goal of home ownership has played a major role. The Canadian domestic economy has evolved so that buying a house or apartment is the major investment for an individual or family. The hope and expectation is that the eventual value of the home will match or outstrip money accumulated in pensions or retirement savings funds. Downsizing after retirement and cashing in on the home is what will make the final decades comfortable and secure. This culture demands that the value of the home rises, and has thus made housing into a speculative commodity. In Canada a house is not a home. It is a slot machine with cooking and sleeping quarters attached.

For most of the last half of the last century, this system functioned well enough. High interest rates on mortgages kept the speculative gambling under control. But in the late 1990s and early 2000s a bubble of get-rich-quick fever took over the housing market. This was driven by several factors, a period of low interest rates chief among them. But this was also the time when Canada got an international reputation as a haven for people from authoritarian states who had made fortunes from their association with the ruling powers and wanted to hide some of their wealth abroad. Canada also looked good to organized criminal cartels that needed to launder their ill-gotten gains. Canada's lack of interest in questioning the origins of money arriving from abroad and its equally intense lack of interest in keeping basic records such as publicly accessible lists of the beneficial owners of real estate, companies, and trusts, made the housing and commercial real estate markets very attractive.

Once foreign money began to drive up prices, it launched a vicious cycle. The value of property in Canada's major cities began to climb more in a year — 30% and more sometimes — than even the most astute stock market investor could hope for. The property market became a feeding frenzy of speculation as Canadians grabbed what looked like a once-in-a-lifetime opportunity to flip themselves up the ladder of ever more valuable property ownership. It quickly became very difficult for governments to know how to respond. At first, they were delighted to grab their cut of the taxes that were due on the ever increasing real estate market activity. It took a while to realise that what was happening was not healthy. But by that time, the frenzy could not be stopped without seriously upsetting the economy and leaving maybe hundreds of thousands of people deeply in debt, sitting on property worth much less than the mortgages they were paying. Governments decided to do nothing, and hope there would not be a catastrophe when interest rates rose, as they inevitably would. Last year, 2023, Canada began to discover the outcome of three decades in the property bubble.

Housing in Canada is a story of two extremes. The lives and prospects of the two groups are profoundly different. A Statistics Canada report in early 2023 found that despite Vancouver being one of the worst cities in Canada to try to find a house or apartment, half of the city's owner-occupied homes were mortgage-free. The owners had paid off the bank and were sitting pretty. People with mortgages are in the other class. The sudden increases in interest rates, launched by the Bank of Canada in 2022 to try to curb inflation, hit many mortgage holders hard and will continue to do so as loans come due for renegotiation. For some people unable to cover the increases in monthly mortgage payments there are foreclosures or forced sales in the offing.

The Canada Mortgage and Housing Corporation reckons that people should have to spend no more than 30% of their monthly income on keeping a roof over their heads, including maintenance and utility costs. In Canada's big cities that's a dream. In Vancouver people buying or renting their homes must pay almost 80% of their monthly income just for their accommodation. In Toronto, the proportion of income is slightly less: 72%. In Saanich, the mixed urban and rural municipality north of Victoria on Vancouver Island, the calculation is that an income of $300,000-a-year is needed to afford a single-family home with a conventional mortgage.

People trying to get into the housing market as either owners or renters face the most daunting prospects. These are usually young people beginning to play their part in adult life, or new immigrants, who the government plans should arrive in Canada at a rate of 500,000-a-year for the foreseeable future. Canada needs to build about 400,000 new homes every year to provide for those trying to find a home, but at the moment it is building just under 300,000. The numbers don't add up. Provincial governments, which have the prime responsibility for trying to find a solution to this problem, show no clear idea of what to do. Both Ontario and British Columbia have passed laws aimed at overriding municipal regulations and practices in an effort to cut red tape for real estate developers. Municipal governments are not happy at being shoved to one side, having their development plans overridden. The unintended consequences will be profound. The need for speed will lead to shortcuts that affect quality and urban planning. Many Canadians have already had the experience of having to spend their life savings on repairing poorly built condominiums. Will that happen again if there is a blind rush to build? The relationship between Canada's municipal governments and real estate developers is already too cozy. It doesn't take much experience or imagination to know that removing regulations and restrictions will give a big boost to corruption.

At the same time, Canada's rental market is not healthy. Owners of rental properties have ridden the coattails of the sales boom. This has made many rents unaffordable and very few properties available for rent as tenants have hung on to what they currently have. There have also been countless incidents of landlords seeking to evict their tenants so they can avoid limits on rent increases and demand vastly inflated monthly payments from new tenants. "Renovictions" — evicting tenants on the grounds that renovations need to be done to the property — are now a common landlord tactic.

The boom and bubble of the last couple of decades made the property market attractive to investors. Figures from Statistics Canada show that across the country more than 20% of all housing is owned by investors. Newly built condominiums have been very attractive to investors over the last few years. The data shows that over a third of all condos in British Columbia are owned by investors, and in Ontario the proportion is even higher; 41.2%. In both those provinces about a third of all new properties, both residential and commercial, built since the turn of the century have been aimed specifically at the investment market. British Columbia is trying to disrupt this market by levying special taxes on the micro apartments aimed at the Airbnb tourist accommodation market. There has been a chorus of outrage from people for whom these little apartments were their main investment, but they have received little public or political sympathy.

There are extrapolations of Statistics Canada data suggesting that over a million houses or apartments are vacant or unoccupied and should, theoretically, be available to people clamouring for accommodation. These numbers are disputed, but in Canada's big cities there are a large number of second homes and apartments that are empty much of the time. Vancouver and Toronto are pressuring the owners of these second homes to rent them out by imposing vacancy taxes on units that are empty for most of the year.

There is no one answer, or even one group of answers for bringing some stability to the Canadian housing market. Higher interest rates will eventually bring a degree of calm, but there will be too many victims from that adjustment who find themselves prisoners of the market or rejected by it. Housing is not only a practical problem of bricks and mortar, it is also an ideological problem. There will be polarized political battles over one very obvious line of attack, which is the building and renting out of publicly owned housing. The federal, provincial, and municipal governments in this country all provide rental housing. Much of it is designed for people who cannot afford housing in the regular market. It is social housing. That doesn't have to be the culture. In several cities in Europe — Stockholm and Vienna come to mind — many of the fine downtown apartments are owned by governments or government-linked institutions and are rented to middle class tenants on long leases. In Singapore people don't own the apartments in which they live. They buy leases, usually for ninety-nine years, either from the government, which owns the property, or the remaining portion of the lease from the previous resident.

It seems very likely that home rental or leasing in going to take on a much larger role in Canadian accommodation culture than it has in the past. Many people choose to be tenants because that's the way they want to live. They don't see renting as a necessary first step on the road to ownership or, in middle age, as an admission of failure. Like many Europeans or Asians, they are happy not to have the responsibility for the structure of their home and are content to manage just their bit of it. As that cohort of lifetime renters grows, there is going to have to be steady municipal and especially provincial attention to landlord-tenant laws and regulations to ensure fairness and stability in the relationship.

All this will become more complex and fraught because of the federal government's intention to increase immigration significantly. That will exert stresses and strains on Canadian society. Ottawa argues that it is essential to welcome these new Canadians in order to sustain the economy. Certainly, there are structural faults in the Canadian economy that put the standard of living for this country's people at risk. The way things are going, we very soon will not be able to afford to live the way we do now. The way we run our economy just won't produce enough to pay for what we want. There is a school of thought in Canada that welcomes the looming shrinkage in consumerism. We should be more concerned with the quality and impact of the things we own and of how we choose to spend our lives rather than rushing to surround ourselves with unnecessary items. A smaller, less consumer-oriented, less environmentally demanding economy would be good for Canada and all of us who live here, goes this argument. Others, of course, see Canada's weak economic growth and all the factors that flow in and out of that reality as a fast-approaching disaster.

There is broad consensus among Canada's business people, plutocrats, and economists about what ails our economy and how to put it on the road to recovery. That consensus was summed up in one word early in 2023 by Thomas d'Aquino, a long-serving head of the Business Council of Canada, and advisor to prime ministers and CEOs for half a century or more. "Complacency," he said.

Complacency is an affliction to which Canadians have become prey, and which can be identified as the cause of several of the problems addressed in this book. In the world of business and the economy, the word sums up the failure to confront a list of problems both homegrown and foreign that have been gathering since the 1980s. It's not a very long list, although over the last decade or so, a small mountain of reports has been published about its key elements and how to deal with them.

The most obvious pressure, even to those outside the worlds of business and economics, is the dramatic growth of Asia as a manufacturing centre for consumer goods. With that rise has come rapid urbanization and the emergence of a consumer middle class in the nations of that region. This fundamental change in the balance of the world's economy away from the countries of the North Atlantic Basin, including Canada, has already set roots in Latin America and is now stretching into Africa. As a relatively small country with an open economy, Canada is dependent on international trade for economic growth. Indeed, trade accounts for 65% of our GDP. The equivalent number is just below 50% in the European Union and 30% in the United States. This makes it imperative that Canada broadens and deepens its trade relationships, but the disaster of its six-decade effort to establish a stable trade relationship with the People's Republic of China has been a vital lesson of how not to do it.

Two-way trade between Canada and the PRC grew to around $90 billion a year by the end of 2018. But that trade was far from balanced. Canada bought around $60 billion a year worth of consumer products and sold about $30 billion of natural resources and agricultural produce, the same brand of exports since trade with the PRC began in 1960. All efforts by Canadian companies to break into the PRC market with manufactured goods or services were blocked by Beijing's state-directed market economy. But Canadian businesspeople and politicians continued to believe they had a special relationship with the PRC, and that just one more push would not only get Canadian companies in on the growth in China, it would also trip the switch for economic and political reform in the PRC. Those delusions came to an end with the Huawei Affair in 2019. Beijing responded violently to the detention of the chief financial officer of Huawei Technologies, Meng Wanzhou, at Vancouver International Airport on a warrant issued by the US Justice Department. Beijing ordered the detention, torture, and conviction on trumped up charges of espionage of two Canadians in China, Michael Kovrig and Michael Spavor. Both men spent over 1,000 days in prison under terrible conditions before they were released in September 2021 when the administration of US President Joe Biden arranged what amounted to a prisoner swap with Meng.

The lessons to Canada of the Huawei Affair were clear, and not only about the hollowness of its relationship with China. Canada cannot have normal trade and diplomatic relations with a regime that takes hostages when there is a problem. But this speaks to a wider lesson. As a relatively small country dependent on trade, Canada needs be careful when deciding which partners to invest in. The story of the Huawei Affair says it is wise to focus on countries with which Canada shares civic, diplomatic, and international security values.

In late 2022, the government produced a new policy on relations with countries in the Indo-Pacific region. This envisaged reaching out beyond China to build trade and diplomatic relations, especially with the democracies of the Indo-Pacific region such as Japan, South Korea, Taiwan, India, and some countries of Southeast Asia. But the new policy came under immediate criticism from people with long experience of Canada-Asia relations. The main reaction was that there did not appear to be sufficient money and other resources committed to make this strategic change work. Convincing commitments about participation in security alliances in the Indo-Pacific region were also missing. As tensions have grown between the PRC, its neighbours such as India, Japan, Taiwan, South Korea, and some of the countries of Southeast Asia, as well as the United States, commitments to joint security are increasingly

seen as a necessary entry fee into broad relations with regional countries. It is notable that Canada has been excluded
from the new naval pact between the United States, the United
Kingdom, and Australia, and also from "The Quad," a security
alliance whose members are India, the United States, Japan,
and Australia. The hard truth is that Canada does not have
the military capacity to play a convincing role in security in
Asia. Canada's military decision-makers remain Eurocentric
in their focus and trade still follows the flag.

At home, Canada has several serious impediments to sustaining sufficient economic growth to maintain the lifestyles
Canadians have come to expect. We have a long-running
problem with productivity. Worker productivity in Canada's
business sector has fallen from close to parity with the United
States in 1984, to barely 70% now. The Organization for
Economic Co-operation and Development reckons that over
the next forty years, Canada will have the lowest growth rate
per capita of any of the thirty-eight countries with developed
economies that it measures. This is not because Canadian
workers are skivers. Far from it. The core of the problem
is bad business decisions, lack of investment, and the influence of foreign ownership. Canadian business managers and
executives have been particularly slow and overly cautious at
investing in information and communications technologies.
These are the new essential infrastructures of business and
productivity, and Canada is lagging because of feeble investment in these areas. Equally timid is Canada's investment in
research and development. Funding for R&D has declined
sharply in recent years and is consistently well below the average among fully industrialized countries. Part of the reason

for this is foreign control of some of Canada's most important businesses. This is particularly noticeable in the foreign
controlled automotive and pharmaceutical sectors. Corporations like to spend their R&D dollars at home, not in their
Canadian outposts.

This lack of R&D spending has had a knock-on effect
and bred widespread hesitancy among Canadian businesses to embrace innovation. There are two main reasons for
this. The first is that while the North American Free Trade
Agreement and its expansion to include Mexico may guarantee open borders for Canadian business, they also dictate the
role that Canada plays. In the relationship with the United
States, Canada is for the most part the supplier of raw materials and partially manufactured goods. With the exception of
the automobile industry, the trade relationship with the US,
and increasingly Mexico, means that the big value-added
parts of the tripartite manufacturing processes don't get done
in Canada.

The second factor influencing Canada's poor record for
innovation is that we are a relatively small market of forty
million people — not much more than the entire population of Tokyo — and our population is dispersed over a vast
geography. More than that, this fragmentation is as much
cultural as it is geographic. Consumer markets across the
country have different likes and dislikes, making innovation
less economically justifiable.

Another reality having a profound influence on Canada's
economic prospect is that we are increasingly a nation of el-
derly people no longer in the work force. In the early 1970s,
when Canada chalked up significant growth in GDP and the

quality of life was expanding on all fronts, there were 6.6 people of working age for every retired Canadian. In other words, there were nearly seven Canadians providing the resources to support the pensions and other services being given to retirees. By 2012 that ratio had declined to 4.2 workers to every retired Canadian, and the predictions are that by 2030 there will be only two working adults for every senior.

Part of the response to this threatening equation is to encourage older people, now benefitting from a life-long health service, to work longer. Very many are happy to do so, not only because they can and like remaining part of the productive community, but also because in economically uncertain times the money is welcome. Far more strategic, however, is the government's program to encourage the immigration of up to 500,000 people a year. These are the people whose work and taxes will change Canada's demographics so that retirees' pensions and care are still affordable.

This influx of people at the rate planned is going to require a massive drive, and not only to build sufficient housing and all the transport and amenities such as power, water supply, and sewage treatment that goes with real estate development. It is going to make equally large demands on Canada's social infrastructure such as schools and healthcare facilities. This in turn will put added pressure on the working relationship between Ottawa and the provinces because providing most of these social services is the responsibility of the provinces. Unless there is federal-provincial foresight and consensus from the start, this drive to increase Canada's population risks becoming a source of constant divisive bickering over who is responsible for what and who pays for what. There are currently few signs of a coordinated plan to prepare for and manage this influx of people. The reality seems to be quite the reverse. Ottawa has let the arrival of temporary foreign workers with residence privileges and students with work permits to get out of hand.

Canada's population increased by 430,635 people in the third quarter of 2023. Of those, 312,758 people, making up 73% of the total, were temporary residents, many of them looking for permanent resident status. As of the end of 2023 there were two-and-a-half million temporary residents in Canada, which is over a million more than there were eighteen months before. They make up more than 6% of Canada's population. To a significant extent this has happened because Ottawa was not paying attention to what other people were doing. The government regulates and sets targets for permanent residents, but it does not control temporary residents. The provinces regulate the colleges and universities that in many cases have come to rely on income from inflated tuition fees charged foreign students. Worse than that, there is evidence that some colleges are little more than false fronts preying on foreign young people who want to get into Canada to work and, perhaps, get permanent resident status.

In January 2024 British Columbia moved against this trafficking. The Post-Secondary Education Minister Selina Robinson announced that no new private colleges or universities would be allowed to enrol international students for two years after their founding. This is part of a package of what she described as "robust safeguards to protect international students against bad actors." A two-year wait before being able to traffic in young workers seems a minimal response. Five years would be a better deterrent.

The federal government is also using its powers to limit what has been called a "student puppy mill." Through 2022 and the first quarter of 2023, Ottawa's Immigration Department approved only 54.3% of the 866,206 applications it received for student visas. More recently, in December 2023, Immigration Minister Marc Miller announced foreign student applicants will have to show that they have at least $20,635 for housing and other expenses, in addition to the money needed to cover one year's tuition fees and travel costs. Later the same month Miller said he plans to control the number of temporary foreign workers coming to Canada in the new year, adding the system has "run a bit rampant for far too long." He said he is particularly concerned about the effects on housing costs of the large influx of students and temporary foreign workers.

Late in 2022, Statistics Canada released a new set of projections based on the government's immigration policy that give a snapshot of the country's multicultural image by 2041; by that year, Canada's population will be 47.7 million people. Twenty-five million of them will either be immigrants or the children of immigrants. Together with their Canadian-born children, this cohort will represent over 52% of the country's population. According to the projection, the current trend of immigration coming from Asia and Africa rather than Europe will continue. By 2041, one-in-four Canadians will have been born either in Africa or Asia. About two in every five Canadians will be a member of a racialized group, which used to be

called "visible minorities." The assumption behind the federal government's policy is that in the future, as in the past,
people from around the world will want to immigrate to Canada. That may no longer be true. There is growing evidence,
mostly anecdotal, that some immigrants are finding Canada
a disappointment. It doesn't live up to its billing as a place of
opportunity for economic advancement or fulfilling career aspirations. Disenchanted immigrants are reported to be leaving
Canada in increasingly large numbers. This is especially true
of the highly qualified immigrants the federal government has
been intent upon attracting. The people who slog it out against
the difficulties of life in Canada are the lesser qualified newcomers, who usually come here first as migrant workers. They
don't have the mobility of better qualified immigrants who can
move relatively easily to other countries when Canada palls.

Canadian immigration policy has aimed for many years
to rob developing countries of their brightest, best, and
best-qualified. It is a policy that many Canadians who have
worked abroad find morally reprehensible. One aspect of
Canada's efforts to snaffle foreign talent had been the opening of Canadian colleges and universities over the last three
decades or so to foreign students. With university and college
placements, foreign students get the opportunity to take out
permanent resident status in Canada. That is the first step on
the way to citizenship. With this prospect, extended families
invest in getting a child to a Canadian college or university
as the path to eventual citizenship for the immediate family.
And that brings us to the next major element in the judgement of the state of wellbeing in Canada; the health of the
education system.

Canada's education system is a strange creature born of the intense religious, cultural, and ethnic divisions among the five communities that came together to form the country in 1867. While it made political sense for Nova Scotia, New Brunswick, Prince Edward Island, and Upper and Lower Canada to form a union in the face of American expansionism, no jurisdiction wanted to give up its individual identity. One of the best ways to ensure the survival of your Catholic or Protestant religion, your Norman and Breton French, or your Acadian, English, Scottish, or Loyalist American heritage was to keep control of how your children were educated; to keep control of the schools. Time and experience has bridged those divisions, but only to a degree. There are still publicly funded religious schools right across the country, and the 1982 Charter of Rights and Freedoms insists that education in French be available in all provinces and territories just as education in English must be on hand in French-speaking Canada for those who want it. This leads to some strange administrative and political constructions of which the situation in Toronto, Canada's largest city, is a slightly extreme, but still representative, example. Toronto has four public school boards operating in the city. They include two English first language school boards: the separate Toronto Catholic District School Board and secular Toronto District School Board. Then there are two French boards, the Catholic Conseil scolaire catholique MonAvenir and the secular Conseil scolaire Viamonde.

Efforts have been made to try to ensure that educational standards and outcomes are consistent across the country; but, with so many cooks stirring the pots, the results are patchy.

Canada's overall education standards suffer. Most organizations ranking the quality of education worldwide put Canada in the top ten, and more frequently in the top five. The claimed literacy and numeracy rate in Canada is just short of universal and about 93% of Canadians get a high school diploma. 68% go on to get a post-secondary degree or diploma. Behind that, however, lie some serious problems. An OECD report in December 2023 said that the overall scores of Canadian students is on a steep downward slide. Scores have declined by 35% between 2003 and 2022. Of great importance in an age of science and technology, only 12% of Canadian students are high achievers at mathematics. This is a jarring contrast with some Asian countries. In Singapore, according to the OECD report, 41% of students are high achievers at maths. The comparable numbers are 27% in Hong Kong and 23% in Japan and South Korea.

The quality and stature of the ministries of education varies significantly from province to province, as does the investment in education. The drive to include children who exhibit learning disabilities or other barriers has also led to what some call the "dumbing down" of academic standards and others describe as simply making success more accessible.

The mélange that makes up the Canadian school stew looks entirely alien, incomprehensible, and therefore problematic to people from countries with unified state education systems. Organizations offering advice to people thinking of immigrating to Canada have picked up on the variations across the country. One such organization in Hong Kong wrote in a recent newsletter:

The disparity in education stems from the differences in education policies and priorities of provinces. Aside from the differences between private and public education that is [sic] familiar to our readers in Hong Kong, Canada also sees disparity within its public education depending on the province you reside in. Whilst primary and secondary education is compulsory and publicly funded across all of Canada, the provinces are responsible for the financial and administrative decisions in education within their jurisdictions.

The newsletter goes on to quote figures published by the Fraser Institute. Per capita annual spending on student education in 2020, said the institute's report, ranged from Alberta at the low end with $12,902 up to Newfoundland's $15,475. The irony here is that because of a provincial emphasis on traditional rote learning, students' exam results in Alberta are generally better than in other provinces.

The Hong Kong newsletter also noted that "Despite strong academic training, Canadian students find it difficult to integrate into the workplace because of the disconnect between education and employment." Moreover, "in the Canadian education system, there is a lack of ample vocational training." The newsletter quoted a Harris Poll from 2020 in which nearly 90% of respondents said they didn't think their education had adequately prepared them for their working lives. That leads to questions that are high in the minds of both providers and consumers of Canada's post-secondary education network: just who and what are Canada's universities and colleges for?

One of the many revelations of the COVID-19 pandemic was just how much colleges and universities have become corporate entities rather than pastures for the nurturing of scholarship and, particularly, the honing of critical judgement skills. For the last couple of decades, governments at all levels have lowered or pegged their funding of universities and colleges. In order to survive, universities and colleges have opened the doors to as many foreign students as they can accommodate. Our tertiary institutions usually charge foreign students three times the tuition fees Canadian students are required to pay. For several of them, this foreign money now represents at least half of their revenue from tuition fees. In Ontario colleges and universities, nearly half of all revenue and third of all students come from abroad.

Until COVID, foreign students appeared happy to pay these fees, though it is worth asking how much the opportunity to acquire Canadian citizenship drove these decisions. Between the years 2000 and 2021 the number of visas issued to foreign students increased by 400%, from 122,665 to 621,565. There was a dip at the height of COVID in 2020 to 528,190 student visas, but in 2022 the number shot up to 807,750. Most foreign students in Canada these days come from India; 319,000 in 2022, with Chinese students second at 100,010. Among all foreign students the focus is on engineering and business administration. Beijing is especially anxious that its students abroad avoid exposure to critical thinking, which is essential to arts degrees. Indeed, the People's Republic of China plants networks of spies among its students abroad to try to ensure they don't pick up any politically dangerous skills.

The bonanza of income for Canadian universities, colleges, and schools from foreign students may well be over. The cost of living in Canada is becoming prohibitive for students from less wealthy countries whose academic success is often an extended family investment. But as a way to prepare foreign students for the reality of Canadian living costs, and to try to end a persistent problem of fraudulent applications, the federal government is requiring applicants to show they can afford to live here before they get a student visa. Until the rules were changed in early December 2023, student applicants had to show they had $10,000 to cover living costs for every year they studied in Canada. That required up-front money has more than doubled to $20,635 a year. Advocates for students expect a sharp drop off in applications by foreign students for whom stumping up $82,540 to cover a four-year course is unworkable.

The drive by higher-education establishments to pack in as many foreign students as they can is not because governments aren't providing funding for tertiary education. They are, but they are making the money available directly to students rather than institutions. There's more political bang for the buck giving the money to individual students rather than to university chancellors to build new facilities. Even so, the average Canadian student gets a bill of at least $30,000 along with their degree and an increasing number are wondering if it's worth it. For three generations or more, a university degree has been the natural aspiration of young Canadians and their parents. And if for their $30,000 they get no more than critical thinking skills, it is probably worth it even now. But the whole design and nature of the Canadian economy, and the workforce that inhabits it is changing rapidly and viscerally. The future is a different country, and we are already seeing glimpses of it.

In 2018, the Royal Bank of Canada commissioned a study that remains a central topic of thought and conversation among people involved in the structure of education and its future. The report looks at what it calls "the coming skills revolution," and addresses the question of "How Canadian youth can thrive in the age of disruption." The opening note by the President and CEO of the bank, Dave McKay, stated that in the year long research project:

> We discovered quite a crisis — of recent graduates who are overqualified for the jobs they're in, of unemployed youth who weren't trained for the jobs that are out there, and young Canadians everywhere who feel they aren't ready for the future of work. Too many have been trained for jobs that may go away rather than equipped with skills that will be ever more valuable.

And there's the key to the findings and recommendations of the report. It concludes that over a quarter of Canadian jobs will be disrupted by technological advances by 2028. Over half the jobs in the Canadian economy will be so disrupted or eradicated by technology that they will require a significant overhaul of the skills required in the workforce. The report states: "Canada's education system, training programs, and labour market initiatives are inadequately designed to help Canadian youth navigate the new skills economy." And, "Canadian employers are generally not prepared, through hiring, training, or retraining, to recruit and develop the skills needed to make their organizations more competitive in a digital economy." Here we have yet more of the complacency of which Thomas d'Aquino spoke.

The RBC report advocates a complete change of approach in thinking about the Canadian job market and the way people move about within it. This revolves around the expectation already noted that Canadians of the generation now entering the workforce will likely have at least a dozen different jobs before they retire. The report suggests that we start thinking about educating young people for a workplace based on six clusters of occupations rather than particular industries. The report contends that many workplace skills equip people to move relatively easily between industries with, perhaps, a minimum of additional training because finding them a new role in the same industry may be impossible. "By focusing on the foundational skills required within each of these clusters, a high degree of mobility is possible between jobs." But the universal qualification everyone must have in the twenty-first century workforce is digital literacy.

The six "clusters" identified in the report are solvers, technicians, crafters, doers, facilitators, and providers. The report runs through the possibilities and opportunities presented by these skill clusters. Solvers, who traditionally include mechanical engineers, architects, and heavy equipment mechanics, should with minimal retraining be able to move into engineering driverless cars, become cloud computing specialists, or big data analysts. Providers can make similar transitions from their current roles as veterinarians, musicians, or child care providers to social media managers, or even lifestyle bloggers. And so on. The core message of the report is that while technologies may change, the essential human skills needed to manage them do not. There is no reason to see again what we saw in the past three or four decades of people being discarded from the work force, with all the personal and community trauma involved, because the industry in which they worked became obsolete. Human skills are always needed. It is just a matter of approaching change and mobility with that clearly in mind.

CHAPTER NINE

Transparency and Trust:
The Essence of Democracy

IN A WELL-ORDERED democracy, transparency and accountability go hand-in-hand. Elected representatives and governments recognize, or should recognize, that they have an
obligation to keep citizens informed about how and why decisions are made in parliament and the legislatures. The duty
to inform is linked to the obligation to accept responsibility
if things go wrong. It may be that a policy was ill-conceived
or badly administered, or it may be that a minister, MP, or
MLA acted unethically. Whatever the case, it is then the duty
of the elected representative to be accountable. Transparency
and accountability are fundamental to the functioning of democracy; without them, there is no reason for the electorate
to have confidence in the system. Today there is a perception
of little willingness among elected politicians to take responsibility for their actions; they shun with equal intensity any
request to be open and honest about how decisions are made.
An essential task for the revitalizing of Canadian democracy
is to bolster both transparency and accountability.

Most mature democracies have freedom of information laws. Sweden was the first country to enact such legislation and it did so in 1766. Since the 1970s similar laws have become an essential element in the bond of mutual trust between a democratically elected government and the citizenry who elected it. It is the demonstration by elected representatives and the governments they run that they are open and transparent in the way they handle the power and responsibilities entrusted to them by voters. Many Canadians probably think we have a Freedom of Information Act, and they may have vague memories of Prime Minister Pierre Trudeau pushing the passage of such an act through Parliament in 1983, shortly before he retired. Yes, he did, but it wasn't a Freedom of Information Act (FIA). It was the Access to Information Act (AIA) — and that is very different breed of cat.

The difference is in the priorities. In an FIA, the aim is that all information about what has happened within government should be made public unless there is good reason not to do so. With access to information legislation, the approach is just the reverse. Everything should be kept confidential and only made public when there are no more excuses for keeping it secret. Moreover, at around the same time that Parliament approved the AIA, it also passed the Privacy Act, which guarantees the privacy of personal information of individuals. Privacy is also a right stipulated in the Charter of Rights and Freedoms, so when there is contest between access to information and privacy of the individual, which is quite often, privacy wins. The result is that while most of our fellow democracies have the right to know what their governments are doing in their name, Canadians do not. Canadians can ask for internal information about decisions made by the government and its departments, but there is absolutely no guarantee they will get it, and if they do get copies of internal documents they are likely to have big chunks of the most informative sections redacted. Secrecy is the default mode for the Canadian government. The federal government has always been that way, but, ironically, the cult of secrecy has become much deeper and more sophisticated since 1983 when the AIA was passed.

The authors of the AIA proclaimed that its purpose was to give the public access to government files. Full stop. And to add to the expectation that this would open a revolution in government transparency, the legislation set out timelines for officials to respond to requests for files. To guarantee this service, it created the Office of the Information Commissioner to investigate complaints. So far so good, but then came the exemptions; the files and information that could not be made public under any circumstances. This has been called the "Mack Truck clause" because of the size of the hole it made in the professions of transparency. Documents that would not be made public included "discussion papers containing background explanations, analysis of problems or policy options, cabinet agendas and minutes, communications between ministers, briefing papers and draft legislation." On top of that, the list of exempted documents included material whose publication could affect federal-provincial relations, information provided to the federal government in confidence by another government, information affecting the safety and security of individuals, information that belonged to private sector companies, and information that could undermine the operations of government. That is only a partial list. And as I have already said, the passage of the Privacy Act in 1983 in tandem with the AIA put further limitations on what information could be supplied to the public.

From the start, AIA was recognized by many as a badly designed and misconceived piece of legislation. The New Democratic Party MP Svend Robinson called it "useless and even more damaging than no bill." John Crosbie, the opposition Conservatives' justice critic, called AIA a gift for "mischief-makers" that would be used only to "embarrass political leaders and titillate the public." Even the first Information Commissioner, Inger Hansen, warned that the act was in danger of becoming an "unwanted offspring of Ottawa."

Most if not all the people who have held the commissioner's post in the last forty years have complained about the way the act is framed, and their own lack of resources and authority to enforce it. A central defect is that the commission has no power to demand compliance if government departments give unsatisfactory reasons for not producing requested information. In her latest report, the current commissioner, Caroline Maynard, said that far too many government departments and institutions seem to consider their compliance with the AIA to be optional. As a result, they don't assign enough staff to the task of processes and responding to requests for information. Over twenty years ago, the then-commissioner, John Reid, said "The Act has now been in operation for almost twenty-one years and, despite its many successes, governments and bureaucrats have still managed to find ingenious ways to wiggle and squirm to avoid the full operation of law."

To a degree, the horror with which civil servants, especially senior figures involved in advising ministers on policy options, regarded the AIA is understandable. Until the 1980s, Canada's civil servants had operated anonymously, as they did in most parliamentary democracies with a professional, non-partisan bureaucracy. Anonymity allowed public servants to give honest advice to their political minister without fear of retribution. The unspoken agreement was that if mistakes were made the minister would take public responsibility. The AIA threatened to remove the protection of anonymity, and the bureaucrats immediately began working on ways to avoid having their names attached to files. One of the first tactics employed was to stop sending written messages. There was a dramatic increase in the amount of government business done on the telephone, which didn't leave a paper trail. When asked to write reports on government activities, some officials took to writing totally bland and unexceptional reports for the public record. Then they would write their real feelings and criticisms in a private letter to the superior who asked for the report. Private correspondence is covered by the Privacy Act. It would never be released.

Fallout from this is that a considerable amount of Canadian history is going unrecorded. The National Archives have found that the volume of files and other material stored with them for safekeeping and as a resource to future historians has decreased markedly.

Senior public servants also found it convenient to get out of the policymaking and advising business as much as they could. Thus, a city full of people whose job is to advise their political masters about policy options have farmed out the job to very expensive private consultants. For every new policy, Canadian taxpayers are paying twice: the civil servants who are employed to do the job, and the private consultants who actually do the work. Early in 2023, questions were raised about the habit of successive governments of hiring outside consultants to develop policy. Total spending on these consultants was over $811 million in the fiscal year 2021 – 22, according to Public Accounts Canada. This is nearly double the $416 million spent six years earlier.

One of the persistent and most reliable tactics to avoid providing requested information is to delay. In the early years after AIA came into force, news reporters leapt on what appeared to be a wonderful opportunity to find out what was really happening in government. The bureaucrats were ready for them. Journalists quickly found that the first line of defence thrown up by the officials responsible for access to information was a precise reading of the question. The journalists' shotgun approach of firing off a general question in the hope that it would produce a large number of files to trawl through usually produced nothing. Indeed, in response to scattergun requests, the officials often delighted in simply sending the press release about the policy in question. Reporters learned the hard way that the only route to real information was to be very precise in wording the question. But that, of course, demanded that the journalist know with a high degree of precision that which he or she was looking for. And for that, the reporter usually needed a source in the department to give advice on how to frame the question that would result in the right answer. It was a cat-and-mouse game from the very start. It continues to be so.

From the beginning, there were efforts to reform the AIA and make it into a proper, functional vehicle for governmental transparency. In 1987, Perrin Beatty, the Solicitor-General in the Conservative government of Prime Minister Brian Mulroney, tabled a report in Parliament with ten recommendations for reforming the AIA and the Privacy Act. It landed with a dull thud and never got up off the floor. In 1998, the Liberal government of Prime Minister Jean Chrétien made minor adjustments. He made it a federal offence to destroy, falsify or conceal public documents, but that had no material effect. In 2000, the government launched an all-out task force review of the AIA. The report was damning, but there was no action. An attempt at reform via a private member's bill in 2003 died on the order paper when the House rose. In 2005 the then-Justice Minister Irwin Cotler published a discussion paper entitled "A Comprehensive Framework for Access to Information Reform." That died with the change of government in 2006.

The new Prime Minister, Stephen Harper, was skeptical about the business of freedom of information. In 2008, his government closed down the central tool for people seeking information, the Coordination of Access to Information Requests System. Harper said the system was too expensive and slowed down the process. The most complete dissection and analysis of the AIA was done in 2008 by several newspapers in partnership with the British Columbia Freedom of Information and Privacy Association. They produced a 393-page report called "Fallen Behind: Canada's Access to Information Act in the World Context." The report concluded that the Canadian law lagged behind most of the sixty-eight countries against which it was measured, and suggested Canada should at least try to have a freedom of information law on par with fellow members of the Commonwealth. When he took office in 2015, Prime Minister Justin Trudeau issued an open letter to Canadians in which he pledged to "set a higher bar for openness and transparency" in Ottawa. "Government and its information must be open by default," he wrote. "Simply put, it is time to shine more light on government to make sure it remains focussed on the people it was created to serve — you."

However genuine the intention, "open by default" has not been obvious in the way the Trudeau government has conducted itself. An unavoidable example is Canada's relationship with the People's Republic of China, which has been a dominant issue since December 1, 2018, when the chief financial officer of Huawei Technologies, Meng Wanzhou, was detained in Vancouver on a warrant issued by the US Justice Department. Precious little information came out of Ottawa for three years, except by leaks, despite Beijing having kidnapped two Canadians (Michael Kovrig and Michael Spavor) and imposed economic sanctions on politically sensitive Canadian exports to China. The crisis in Ottawa-Beijing relations became of heightened interest when new confirmations were released from within government of the extent to which the Chinese Communist Party (CCP) had infiltrated Canadian public life. This included Beijing's attempts to influence the outcome of elections in constituencies with a large population of Canadians of Chinese heritage, its control over almost all

Chinese language media in Canada, the use of surreptitious means to donate money to favoured candidates and to the Trudeau Foundation in the belief this could influence government, and even its establishment of police stations in Canada to survey and intimidate Chinese Canadians.

In all these cases, the federal government's default position was secrecy when it can be argued that transparency is the most powerful and the cleanest weapon Canada has to confront and defeat infiltration and influence-peddling by the CCP or any other nation. It is not only Beijing that seeks to influence politics and public discourse in Canada. Many immigrants to Canada are dissidents in their home countries. Some continue their political activities after their arrival in Canada, and it is natural that the governments of their former homelands like to keep an eye on what is happening. India, Iran, Russia, and Sri Lanka are just as interested as the Chinese government in what their former nationals are saying and doing here. It is not always governments that have an unhealthy desire to manipulate public affairs in Canada. Most notable are non-governmental organizations and interest groups from all aspects of the political spectrum in the US that give funds or otherwise support like-minded groups in Canada.

It should not be a surprise that, when a new party forms the government, its mentality is still in opposition mode, and it remains in favour of transparency. But once they've got their collective knees under the desks in the corner offices of power, their worldview changes. Yet, it cannot be beyond the wit of legislative lawyers to draft a freedom of information act that protects civil servants from being pilloried in public, placing the responsibility for government actions with the ministers in charge, giving the freedom of information commissioner authority to demand answers from departments, and still gives the public the right to see what their government is up to and why. Many other countries do it, and only the deeply embedded culture of secrecy prevents Canada from doing the right thing.

But, as I wrote at the beginning of this chapter, transparency, or the lack of it, walks arm-in-arm with accountability. If successive federal governments have failed to make openness and transparency their default positions, they have been equally derelict on accountability. No longer do members of parliament resign for transgressions, no matter how unethical. In part, this is a result of the polarization of Canadian politics, a disease caught from the disintegration of democracy south of the border. It also comes from the locker-room, politics-as-sport cultures, and the dominance of celebrity. Winning is everything. Never apologize. Never admit defeat.

The records of Justin Trudeau and Stephen Harper before him are full of abuses of power and scandals which at other times in Canada and in other parliamentary democracies today would have at least caused the resignation or ouster of the prime minister, and probably triggered elections. There are distinct stylistic differences in the abuses, though one influences the other. The Liberals' transgressions usually stem from a sense of entitlement. They have come to believe that a Liberal government in Ottawa is the natural order of things. This inevitably breeds a culture where ethics are of secondary importance. Moral transgressions can be ignored or shuffled into the background because unless the Liberal Party has real problems, the Conservatives cannot win enough votes in the right parts of the country to win power in Ottawa. The Liberal Party, therefore, has a great deal of leeway — a lot it can get away with before it angers enough voters to risk defeat at the polls.

The ethical failings of the Harper government from 2006 to 2015 came from paranoia flowing from the belief that the Liberals have been the natural party of power in Canada since Confederation. On occasions when the Conservatives manage to win office, they are constantly on edge. This syndrome was more evident in the Harper years than in the tenure of some of his Conservative predecessors, especially Brian Mulroney. Harper acted as though he believed the entire public service had been brainwashed and indoctrinated with Liberal Party attitudes. He appeared to think the public service was out to get his Conservative government and would grab any opportunity to embarrass him. Harper's strategy, such as it was, was to try to exorcise the public service and to cleanse it and Parliament of what he saw as Liberal Party culture. In its place he tried to instill Conservative sympathies and methodologies. A more subtle and secure personality might have succeeded, but Harper had neither of those qualities. His nine years in office was peppered with abuses that fall roughly into two categories. One was playing fast-and-loose with the parliamentary and governmental system to make it possible for Harper to get his way. The other was clumsy corruption.

Harper was the first Canadian Prime Minister to be found in contempt of Parliament. In 2011, Speaker Peter Milliken ruled that the Conservative government was in contempt of Parliament on two occasions. In one case, the minister for international aid had lied about the circumstance surrounding the defunding of a charitable organization. A second verdict of contempt was issued by the Speaker for the government's refusal to reveal the costs of tax cuts, criminal justice measures, and the troubled F-35 fighter jet program.

One of Harper's first quests after coming to office in 2006 was to try to pack the Senate with Conservative appointees. This did not go well. In 2013 the Senate Committee on Internal Economy announced there would be a forensic audit of the expenses of four Tory Senators: Mike Duffy, Pamela Wallin, Mac Harb, and Patrick Brazeau. All four were subsequently suspended from the Senate over allegations of improper claims. Duffy and Brazeau also faced criminal charges. Duffy was eventually acquitted of the charges and those against Brazeau were dropped.

Allegations of attempts to manipulate elections dogged Harper from the beginning. In the 2006 election, the Conservative Party pled guilty to exceeding the limits on campaign advertising. In 2011 a Conservative organizer was convicted of sending out robocalls to likely Liberal and New Democratic Party voters directing them to the wrong polling stations. In the 2008 election, Conservative MP Dean Del Mastro was convicted of breaking spending rules. Illegal campaign donations forced Labrador MP Peter Penashue to quit Harper's Cabinet in 2013.

Harper lost his foreign affairs minister Maxime Bernier in 2008 when he was forced to resign after it was revealed he had inadvertently left classified North Atlantic Treaty Organization (NATO) documents at the home of his girlfriend, Julie Couillard, who had past links to biker gangs. In

2018 Bernier left the Conservative Party, saying it was "too intellectually and morally corrupt to be reformed." He created the ultra-rightwing People's Party of Canada (PPC). In the 2021 election the PPC got almost 5% of the votes, winning no seats. This was up from 1.6% of the popular vote in the 2019 election.

Canada was part of the international coalition trying to eradicate terrorists and extremists from Afghanistan in 2009 when a senior Canadian diplomat told a parliamentary committee that insurgents detained by the Canadian forces and transferred to the local authorities were almost certainly being tortured. The committee demanded documents referring to the allegations, which the Harper government refused to provide. Instead, Harper used an old but seldom used procedure and persuaded Governor General Michaelle Jean to prorogue Parliament — close the current parliamentary session early — in order to halt the committee's work. Harper had used the prorogation ploy the year before in 2008 when it was clear the minority Conservative government was about to be defeated by a coalition of the Liberal, NDP, and Bloc Québécois opposition parties.

A couple of other scandals were just run-of-the-mill corruption. In 2010, Cabinet Minister Tony Clement took advantage of the upcoming summit of the G8 group of leading industrialized countries at Huntsville in his Muskoka riding to grab $50 million for legacy projects. An investigation by the Auditor General found there had been little or no oversight about how the money had been doled out, and that municipalities far away from the meeting site in Huntsville had been given hundreds of thousands of dollars for parks, sidewalk repair and, famously, for the construction of a gazebo. Also in 2010, the Defence Minister Peter MacKay called for a search and rescue Cormorant helicopter to come to pick him up from a private fishing lodge in Newfoundland at an estimated cost to the public purse of $16,000.

The election of the Liberals led by Justin Trudeau in 2015 was at first widely viewed as a generational change and a new dawn in Canadian politics at a time when the US was embroiled in the uncertainties of Donald Trump's drive for the Republican Party's presidential nomination and campaign for the White House. Conflicts of interest are the Liberals' speciality in the breeches-of-ethics stakes. Trudeau had not been long in power when he was censured by the Ethics Commissioner for accepting a free Christmas holiday for his family and friends on a private Caribbean Island owned by the Aga Khan. There was another criticism from the Ethics Commissioner two years later in 2019. The commissioner ruled that Trudeau violated the Conflict of Interest Act when he pressured his Attorney-general, Jody Wilson-Raybould, to defer corruption charges against SNC-Lavalin, a Québec-based multinational engineering company. Then, in late 2022, the Minister of International Trade, Mary Ng, was found to have contravened the Conflict of Interest Act by giving two contracts worth nearly $23,000 to a public relations firm owned by her good friend and Liberal Party strategist, Amanda Alvaro. Ethics Commissioner Mario Dion also censured former Finance Minister Bill Morneau, Trudeau's Parliamentary Secretary Greg Fergus, and Intergovernmental Affairs Minister Dominic LeBlanc for ethical transgressions.

This last act by Dion, who resigned in February 2023 for health reasons, highlights the perils of incestuous politics and the problems of a small gene pool of talent in a company town like Ottawa. To fill the gap until a new full-time Ethics Commissioner could be appointed, Trudeau picked Intergovernmental Affairs Minister LeBlanc's sister-in-law Martine Richard. Greg Fergus is another example of the limited choices available in Ottawa. He has been a professional Liberal since being selected as president of the party's youth wing in the mid-1990s. In 2007, then-leader Stephane Dion appointed him national director of the Liberal Party. Fergus is credited with creating the party in its current form. He was elected to Parliament in 2015 and has been one of the most effective and enthusiastic partisans on the Liberal benches. With his record of having been rebuked for a conflict of interest and his intense party loyalty, Fergus did not seem an obvious candidate for Speaker of the House following predecessor Anthony Rota's resignation after honouring a man who fought for a Nazi unit during the Second World War. But Fergus was elected on October 3, 2023. He managed to cause more outrage and raise questions about his suitability when, in December 2023, he appeared in a leadership convention video paying tribute to the interim leader of the Ontario Liberal Party, John Fraser. In the video, Fergus appeared from the Speaker's Chamber dressed in his full rig as Speaker of the House of Commons, a role that is meant to be beyond partisan politics. There were calls for his resignation. He did not oblige.

The implications of the culture of secrecy in Ottawa are profound. It is nearly impossible to put a number on it, but there can be no question that government secrecy and refusal to be accountable for its actions are playing a significant part in public scepticism about the federal government and all its works. The institutional lack of transparency and accountability is a major reason why so many Canadians feel isolated from and unrepresented by the country's establishment.

Measure Twice, Cut Once

ALL DEPRECIATION REPORTS contain maintenance projects that are not urgent and can be set aside for later. Canada has plenty of those. What cannot be deferred is repair and the necessary rebuilding of the structure of the house. It will not continue to stand otherwise.

In my opinion, Canada is at the point in the life of its political and social construction where two load-carrying beams in the structure need urgent attention. One of them is the need to revive Canadians' trust in the political system. There is a need to restore their belief that our democracy is effective in representing them and working for their objectives. The second is the economy. This too needs serious remodelling so that it restores equity to the distribution of wealth and rebuilds the confidence for Canadians that they can aspire to a better standard of living. Unless these two deficits are tackled and tackled soon, the lesson from other democracies that have stumbled in recent years is that Canada will fall prey to glib demagogues and populists who stir up the population's anger and anxieties to feed their own ambitions for power. That is the road that leads first to the end of a tolerant society and then on to some form of authoritarianism.

Restoration of confidence in the political system needs to address the workings of Parliament and the template for elections. The fabric of Parliament is corroded at several crucial joints. The political parties no longer function effectively; they have allowed themselves to be overtaken by the culture of celebrity and are fixated on image at the expense of substance. They have become consumed with the passion to win power, forgetting the real purpose of forming a government. Parties need to reform the way in which they select their leaders and how they remove them so that the chosen person remains beholden to the members of their caucus and thus parliament. This will erode and hopefully end the culture of celebrity leadership. It will make parliament what it is meant to be: the forum of representatives elected by voters to pursue their constituents' wellbeing and not the often bitterly divided, ill-mannered, and angry cockpit of fan clubs that it is now. That in turn should attract candidates from a variety of backgrounds and expertise who genuinely want to serve their communities rather than the professional partisans who increasingly dominate the benches of the House of Commons now.

The authority of parliament that has been handed to the Supreme Court, because of the introduction forty years ago of the Charter of Rights and Freedoms, must be restored. Current indications are that this problem may sort itself out because of the number of provinces invoking Article 33, the notwithstanding clause, in legislation they think may be challenged by the court.

Once the supremacy of parliament is established, other necessary reforms should fall into place. The workings of parliament itself should again become the preserve of MPs and the stage management of the prime minister and the Prime Minister's Office should end. The next task should be to end as far as is feasible the patronage power of the prime minister. Independent commissions can be established, as in other parliamentary democracies, to manage appointments to senior posts in crown corporations and the selection of deputy ministers in the civil service. Finding a new and acceptable way to choose the head of state — the Governor General — will require some thought and discussion. It will be difficult because the natural inclination of Canadian voters will be to have a direct election for the position. That must be avoided because it would give the Governor General personal independent political legitimacy, likely undermining the supremacy of Parliament. Canada and Australia have both experienced constitutional crises when governors general appointed by Britain tried to dictate to parliament. These are damaging and unnecessary clashes that must be avoided. There are several options for selecting candidates for the Governor General's job, but the final choice should probably be made by a free vote in the House of Commons.

Similar reforms should apply to the selection of lieutenant governors in the provinces. And while the corrosion of the workings of the provincial legislatures is not as advanced as it is in the House of Commons, all of them need to take a clear-eyed look at their deficiencies, especially in those provinces where low voter turnout suggests lack of public confidence in their political institutions.

Provinces have already done much more than federal politicians to explore new election models in which the outcomes better reflect the will of the people. There is a balance that must be found here. The system adopted must produce a fairer outcome than the current first-past-the-post method, but also render a verdict that creates a working government. The experiences of countries that use proportional representation systems is that all too often it takes weeks, months, and even years for parties to negotiate a governing coalition. These alliances are often unstable, sometimes leading to repeat elections that also fail to produce a government. PR systems tend to be consumed by politics, with the business of government and administration, which ought to be the dominate purpose of the election process, being almost an afterthought. PR systems tend to give far too much power and influence to fringe and extremist parties. There is plenty of evidence of this in Europe and elsewhere. The best improvement on FPTP is a ranked ballot system that requires voters to pick candidates in order of preference. If no candidate wins a majority on the first count, voters' second and third choices are distributed until one candidate has majority support.

I also think that Canada should require citizens to vote in elections at all levels, and fine those people who do not. Canadian citizenship comes overloaded with rights. It should also come with more responsibilities than it does at the moment.

Canada doesn't have the same degree of control over its economy as it does over its political culture. The curse of geography is part of the reason for Canada's limited economic autonomy. Like it or not, Canada cannot escape the gravitational pull of the world's largest economy south of our border. Efforts to do just that by imposing a degree of protectionism —

justified as defence of cultural individuality — have a profound economic impact. A very high cost of living premium goes with living in Canada. Geography also has given Canada a vast, resource-rich landmass with, so far, a relatively small population. This is a blessing and a curse. Trade in resources provides Canada with fundamental economic stability, but it also fosters a business culture of complacence. Canadians don't know how to compete in the international marketplace. At home, the big beasts among Canadian companies don't have to compete. Far too many of them are oligopolies that dominate their markets with little or no competition.

Canada's four biggest banks hold three-quarters of domestic deposits. Loblaws and Sobeys sell 34% of Canada's groceries. There are only two significant airlines, Air Canada and WestJet. Canadians pay more for Internet and cellphone connections than their North Atlantic neighbours because there are only three suppliers in the market. The main reason for these near-monopolies is that successive governments have refused to block mergers that smother competition. On the other hand, Canadian governments have always been swift to prohibit foreign investment that might benefit consumers. Of the thirty-eight members of the Organization for Economic Cooperation and Development (OECD) only New Zealand, Iceland, and Mexico are less open to foreign investment. Canada also comes very low in the OECD's league table for spending on research and development. Canada spends only 1.7% of gross domestic product on R&D, well shy of the 2.7% OECD average. And for a country that considers itself tech savvy, Canada doesn't make much of a show on the international marketplace. Among OECD countries, cutting edge technology products such as computers and pharmaceuticals make up 7% of their exports on average. In Canada it is only 4% of exports. Then there is the wealth disparity, which has been growing since the 1970s, and the standard of living for most Canadians, which has been static for the same period.

It has taken Canada forty years to get into this mess. So the necessary reawakening of economic culture is going to take some time, and is going to require persistent leadership. We don't have a good record for sticking with a program or keeping an objective in clear sight, so it is hard to be optimistic. The most that can be hoped for are moves towards rebalancing Canada's economic culture so that those people who have been sidelined for the last four decades — the bulk of the population — get a fairer deal. That should be the priority.

The rebalancing needs to recognize that the power and remuneration for investors and managers in the quadrilateral relationship of corporations and institutions is seriously damaging the lives of the other two partners: employees and customers. Many things can be done to remove the unhealthy distortions in our economy. A minimum wage should be a living wage. The introduction of a guaranteed annual income for Canadians has backing from several influential advocates, but the only attempt at a proper test of its effectiveness, conducted in Ontario, was aborted by Premier Doug Ford. There should be standard tests of the idea of a guaranteed annual income in each of Canada's regions so that its strengths and weaknesses can be properly judged. Legislation requiring profit-sharing with employees should be pursued, both for its economic good and for the restoration of a culture of mutual respect between employees and corporate managers. It is extraordinary that a country so dedicated to free trade in international commerce has yet to establish free trade within Canada. Some efforts have been made in this area, and there have been some achievements, but the barriers to trade and the easy movement of residence for Canadians between provinces remains bewildering. Governments at all levels should also put far more muscle behind programs to encourage research and development in Canada, and to boost incentive programs for investment. Serious efforts need to be made to break up the near-monopolies that promote profiteering in businesses such as banking, communications technology, grocery sales, and air transport.

Canada is not broken, but with every year that passes the creaks of protest in the strained joints of its political and social construction get louder and louder. Nearly a quarter of a century ago Jeffrey Simpson, *The Globe and Mail*'s former national affairs columnist, ended his book *The Friendly Dictatorship* with a characteristically gentlemanly exhortation to Canadians. If Canadians have true affection and commitment to their troubled political system, he wrote, they can change and improve it. But he warned that, "Apathy and cynicism are soulmates. They are on the rise, but they are democracy's foes, and as such, worth combating."

Simpson was right. Because of apathy and the growth of cynicism about politics in the last twenty-five years the state of our nation is much more perilous today than the country he described at the turn of the century. The time for being polite about our predicament is long passed. The time for a true reform movement is now. If that does not happen, a writer who in twenty-five year's time produces a similar book to this one will be describing a broken country, a house collapsed in upon itself, the result of unnecessary and cowardly neglect.

ACKNOWLEDGEMENTS

THIS BOOK HAS direct lineage from my 2020 book *Restoring Democracy in an Age of Populists and Pestilence*. That book was published by Cormorant Books in the middle of the first year of COVID-19, and it dealt with the pressures that had eroded democracy since the end of the Cold War in the countries bordering the North Atlantic. Trying to get public interest in the book was difficult to say the least when people could not gather for the usual book tour events. Attention gathering was done on Zoom, and it quickly became apparent to me that the normal offering of an author on these occasions — a succinct summation of the book with enough tabloid flare to encourage the audience to rush to the book-buying table at the back of the room — didn't work in that medium.

What it does encourage, however, is an interview or discussion format. The seeds of this book were sown by the many people who took part in my 2020 Zoom-fests and who offered their own observations or comments about the state of Canadian democracy. In addition to that small host of people in the many organizations with which I had Zoom meetings is a coterie of my friends and acquaintances with whom I discussed and debated the issues in this book over coffee. Because this is a polemic and I know that several of them disagree with my point of view on several issues, I want to make it crystal clear that the thoughts in this book are mine and mine alone. But my friend Ken Robson and my cousin John Manthorpe merit special thanks for engaging with my stream of consciousness diatribes at our regular meetings over coffee, and for their sage comments on early drafts of the manuscript.

Marc Côté, my editor and publisher at Cormorant Books in Toronto, prodded me into writing this book. Both of us felt *Restoring Democracy* was the prelude and scene-setter for an examination of the state of Canadian democracy. Marc is a superb editor and a pleasure to work with. Thanks also to Barry Jowett, Sarah Cooper, Sarah Jensen, Marijke Friesen, and Fei Dong at Cormorant for their work in the design and production of the book.

This is the sixth book I have written during the years of my life and partnership with Petrina. Her support and comfort is indispensable.

Jonathan Manthorpe is the author of four books on international relations, politics, and history, including the national bestseller and *Globe and Mail* Top 100 Books of 2019, *Claws of the Panda: Beijing's Campaign of Influence and Intimidation in Canada*. His previous books include *Forbidden Nation: A History of Taiwan* and *The Power and the Tories: Ontario Politics 1943 to the Present*. In recent years he has written columns for a wide variety of publications in Canada and overseas. Over his fifty-year career as a journalist, he has been the foreign correspondent in Asia, Africa, and Europe for Southam News, the European Bureau Chief for the *Toronto Star*, and the national reporter for *The Globe and Mail*. In 1981 and 1982, Manthorpe was an advisor in London to Prime Minister Pierre Elliott Trudeau on the patriation of the Canadian constitution. For the last few years, he has been based in Victoria, British Columbia.

We acknowledge the sacred land on which Cormorant Books operates. It has been a site of human activity for 15,000 years. This land is the territory of the Huron-Wendat and Petun First Nations, the Seneca, and most recently, the Mississaugas of the Credit River. The territory was the subject of the Dish With One Spoon Wampum Belt Covenant, an agreement between the Iroquois Confederacy and Confederacy of the Ojibway and allied nations to peaceably share and steward the resources around the Great Lakes. Today, the meeting place of Toronto is still home to many Indigenous people from across Turtle Island. We are grateful to have the opportunity to work in the community, on this territory.

We are also mindful of broken covenants and the need to strive to make right with all our relations.